Contents

Acknowledgements

Crown copyright material is reproduced with the permission of the controller of Her Majesty's Stationery Office.

I wish to thank:

All the children I have taught in Bradford and Leeds who have been a constant inspiration. In particular, those children (and their parents) who have permitted me to use photographs and examples of their work in this book.

Caroline Hennigan, Linda Walker and Helen Price, with whom I have enjoyed working and from whom I have learnt so much.

Leeds Education Authority Early Years Development Team for their role in my professional development.

The Elisabeth Svendsen Trust for Children and Donkeys for granting permission to use their name, and a photograph of their staff and one of their donkeys, in chapter 4.

The following colleagues and friends for their professional and moral support during the writing of this book: Jane Barnfield, Chris Barnfield, Mona Fairholme, Jo Kurasinski, Susan Buxey and Claire Clements.

My family, in particular my husband, Fred, for his unfaltering support; my Mum, Helen Sefton, for her practical help and confidence in me, and my sister, Sarah, for her encouragement.

Preface

As we enter an exciting time of development in early years provision, practitioners from a wide variety of settings, bringing a range of strengths, training and experience to the foundation stage, are linked by a common aim – to offer our young children learning opportunities and experiences of the highest possible quality, while ensuring that the care and curriculum they receive are appropriate to their needs and stage of development.

As a practising nursery teacher I am well aware of the challenges that face practitioners in providing a high-quality curriculum for very young children. However, I remain convinced that careful and thorough planning is crucial in effecting good educational practice. I also recognise the need for practical support material in which ideas are easily transferable and activities proven to be successful.

In this book I aim to offer the busy practitioner clear guidance on planning children's play and learning in an exciting environment, and to provide a bank of 'tried and tested' ideas and plans. All plans identify key areas of learning and are linked to early learning goals in these areas. I have used photographs of children at play and examples of their work to illustrate the text and, I hope, bring plans to life.

The book is intended as a resource for colleagues already working with children in the foundation stage, and as a useful support to those still training. Choosing to work with young children destines us to much hard work and some inevitable heartache, but for me there is no other choice – the joy of sharing in children's delight at their discoveries more than compensates for the exhaustion felt at the end of the day! I trust that the activities included in the book will be enjoyed by both children and adults.

Jane Drake
December 2000

Introduction

Adults who criticise teachers for allowing children to play are unaware that play is the principal means of learning in early childhood. It is the way through which children reconcile their inner lives with external reality. In play, children gradually develop concepts of causal relationships, the power to discriminate, to make judgements, to analyse and synthesise, to imagine and to formulate. Children become absorbed in their play and the satisfaction of bringing it to a satisfactory conclusion fixes habits of concentration which can be transferred to other learning.

(Department of Education and Science 1967, para 523)

The inclusion of all reception children in the foundation stage (introduced in September 2000) has implications for practitioners in reception classes and all other settings. Reception teachers are released from planning to the age-related Desirable Outcomes[1] for some children, and to the National Curriculum for others. All children, from the age of three to the end of the reception year, are part now of a continuous stage. Some of the expectations defined in the early learning goals have consequently been pushed further along the developmental pathway, with the result that there is a greater distance between the point at which three-year-olds join the setting and the goals.

There is an urgent need, then, for practitioners to understand the stages of learning through which children pass in order to assess their needs and plan accordingly. In May 2000 the Department for Education and Employment (DfEE) issued *Curriculum Guidance for the Foundation Stage* (QCA 2000), which offers practitioners a breakdown of the goals and broad expectations for children at different developmental stages. Activities and learning experiences that take place in the early years setting should enable children to make progress on the 'learning journey' through the bands of 'stepping stones' towards, and sometimes beyond, the early learning goals.

In addition to being familiar with 'sequential patterns of development' (Department of Education and Science 1990), there needs to be a clear perception by practitioners of the characteristics of young children as learners. How children learn is a complex issue and precise definitions elusive, but it is necessary to identify features of effective learning before discussing ways of planning content and mode. Julie Fisher (1996) offers clarification of this matter, suggesting that young children learn by 'being active', 'organizing their own learning experiences', 'using language' and 'interacting with others'.

---

[1] A set of expectations for children, on reaching statutory school age the term after their fifth birthday, published in the document superseded by the early learning goals.

These four significant aspects of learning are evident in the other reports and studies, for example, the Rumbold Committee (Department of Education and Science 1990) recognised that:

- 'Learning should be primarily first-hand, experiential and active. Young children need opportunities and space to explore and discover'.
- 'Children's independence and autonomy needs to be promoted. Children should be encouraged to take responsibility for their learning'.
- 'Talk is central to the learning process. It should be reciprocal and often initiated and led by the child'.
- 'Young children are social beings and learning should take place in a social context'.

It is over three decades since the Plowden Committee (Department of Education and Science 1967) acknowledged the importance of play, and defined its role, in the learning process. Although, during that time, initiatives in education have been many, and debates over the content and delivery of the curriculum vociferous, play is still valued as a way in which young children learn and promoted as an appropriate context in which to embed the early years curriculum.

The QCA's explanation of the benefits of play in *Curriculum Guidance for the Foundation Stage* clearly reiterates some of the points made in the Plowden report. When considered in the light of earlier definitions of the means by which learning takes place, this explanation provides a very strong case for planning a curriculum rich in play opportunities:

Through play, in a secure environment with effective adult support, children can:

- Explore, develop and represent learning experiences that help them make sense of the world
- Practise, and build up ideas, concepts and skills
- Learn how to control impulses and understand the need for rules
- Be alone, be alongside others or cooperate as they talk or rehearse their feelings
- Take risks and make mistakes
- Think creatively and imaginatively
- Communicate with others as they investigate or solve problems
- Express fears or relive anxious experiences in controlled and safe situations.

(QCA 2000)

Also emphasised in the document is the notion that play and work are indistinguishable to the young child. This, again, is not a new concept. Susan Isaacs (1929), in her book *The Nursery Years*, stated that: 'Play is indeed the child's work, and the means whereby he grows and develops.' So, play should not be seen by the adult as a separate activity. For children, it is an integral, and necessary, part of their lives in the setting, and at home. Through play and first-hand experiences, children are motivated to learn and their learning needs can be identified and met.

However, it is not enough to simply subscribe to the 'learning-through-play' philosophy. Free play in an ill-equipped environment with little thought given to the opportunities and support offered is not guaranteed, or even likely, to lead to appropriately challenging learning experiences for all children. For experiences of the highest quality to take place, children's play and learning needs to be carefully planned. This does not necessarily mean that practitioners will directly plan the content, or specific outcome, of play, although a more focused approach to activities is sometimes appropriate. Rather they will create a fertile environment (including quality provision and adult support) that enables children to flourish as active learners through play.

The early learning goals set expectations for children's achievements by the end of the reception year, 'but are not a curriculum in themselves' (QCA 2000). It is the responsibility of the practitioner to plan opportunities that will enable children to make progress in their learning.

It is worth determining at this stage what is understood by the term 'curriculum'. The very word has, historically, been more usually associated with prescribed frameworks for education in schools but, for foundation-stage children, is defined by the QCA (2000) as 'everything children do, see, hear or feel in their setting, both planned and unplanned'.

In accepting this broad definition, practitioners should recognise the diversity of children's learning and acknowledge that their learning is not always confined to what has been directly planned, or intended, by the adult. They must also take into account the range of experiences and interests children bring to the setting. If a programme is to be effective in motivating children and in promoting meaningful, cross-curricular learning, there must be flexibility and a 'built-in' system of evaluation which feeds into the planning process, enabling practitioners to identify, and respond to, individual interests and needs.

Although it is important to appreciate that learning is a continuous and accumulative process and does not begin or end in 'key stages', it should also be pointed out that the curriculum provided for children in the foundation stage, whichever early years setting they attend, will certainly be different to that offered to older children. However, while a curricular framework in the foundation stage may be more 'concealed', and learning less discrete, it is nonetheless essential in order to provide a structure for planning and assessment of children's learning. The six areas of learning (as defined by QCA 2000) serve as a basic structure around which to plan experiences and activities:

- Personal, social and emotional development
- Communication, language and literacy
- Mathematical development
- Knowledge and understanding of the world
- Physical development
- Creative development.

In conclusion, and as an introduction to the main content of the book, the following summary is offered. The aim of the foundation-stage educator is to provide a broad and balanced curriculum, and opportunities that will enable all children to develop knowledge, concepts, skills and attitudes. This learning will often take place in the context of purposeful play, and always in a meaningful situation. Children will access the curriculum through a well-planned and appropriately resourced learning environment that takes account of the characteristics of young children as learners, and the developmental course they take.

Remaining chapters focus on the challenging task facing practitioners in planning and supporting such a curriculum.

Those adults who are sufficiently open-minded to let themselves be guided by children will be able to see children exercising control over their world through play.

(Hurst 1991)

CHAPTER 1

Planning the learning environment and quality areas of provision

For children to have rich and stimulating experiences, the learning environment should be well planned and well organised. It provides the structure for teaching within which children explore, experiment, plan and make decisions for themselves, thus enabling them to learn, develop and make good progress.

(QCA 2000)

The content of this chapter is organised as follows:

Provision in the learning environment

The environment that is created in the early years setting should be exciting to children, inspiring in them an eagerness to explore and a zest for learning. Quality provision serves to support and challenge young children in their development across all areas of learning. Through the learning environment, and supported by the practitioner, all children can access a broad and balanced curriculum and make progress from their own starting point towards the early learning goals and beyond.

When planning the curriculum, the practitioner needs to give consideration to which 'areas' should be included in the basic provision. The physical characteristics of the setting will influence decisions in terms of facilities and equipment available, and it may be that restricted space does not allow practitioners to offer the range of provision on a daily basis that they would choose in an ideal world. In the case of limited space, practitioners will need to plan carefully to ensure that the permanent provision (i.e. the provision offered to children every day) covers the basic curriculum and that the learning environment is enhanced regularly through the addition of extra resources (perhaps on a rotational basis) and the planning of focus activities (see chapter 2) in order to further develop and extend children's learning in certain areas.

The following areas of provision are recommended for inclusion:

- Role-play areas
- Construction area
- Mark-making/office area
- Maths area
- Water area
- Sand areas (wet and dry sand)
- Workshop area
- Malleable materials area (clay, dough, etc.)
- Music area (making and listening to music)
- Painting area
- Book 'corner'
- IT area.

There should also be regular opportunities planned, and appropriate equipment available, for baking and various other food preparation activities.

Equipment for practising and developing physical skills such as climbing and balancing should be part of the permanent provision, and a list of suggested resources is included later in this chapter (see p. 37).

The role of the adult in supporting learning

The role of the adult is crucial in identifying children's needs, assessing their stage of development and intervening in play to support individuals in moving forward. The timing and nature of such interventions will greatly influence the quality of the learning experiences that take place within the environment. Practitioners need to plan to spend time in areas of provision (perhaps at a focus activity, see chapter 2), observing and engaging in play, and also to involve themselves in, and respond to, children's play spontaneously.

In her book, *The Nursery Teacher in Action*, Margaret Edington (1998) writes about 'enabling children to learn'. Her explanation of the role of the teacher in supporting children's learning can be applied to all practitioners working in early years settings.

Teachers enable each child to learn and develop by helping them to sustain their current interests, and also by interesting them in new things. The role of the enabler involves her in using a number of teaching roles and strategies. Sometimes she initiates experiences with a view to stimulating, supporting or extending interest. Sometimes she acts as a role model for the children to encourage particular kinds of dispositions or skills. Sometimes she demonstrates skills or imparts knowledge. Often she uses a combination of these strategies. Whichever approach she uses, she keeps the needs of the children in mind to help her determine the optimum moment for learning – the moment when the child wants to, or needs to, learn.

(Edington 1998)

In order for the practitioner to fulfil these aspects of the role effectively, provision must be planned carefully, giving thought to all areas of learning, and the full range of needs within the setting.

Planning the environment

In planning the environment, it may help practitioners to view provision as a structure that scaffolds children's learning but also allows them the freedom to experiment, investigate and pursue personal interests. Children should be encouraged to become active and independent learners and feel confident in 'trying out' ideas in a supportive and 'safe' climate. Provision should be organised in a way that offers children opportunities for working individually, in pairs or groups, with an adult and for observation of other children at play. It should be constant enough for children to return to areas over a period of days or weeks to develop ideas and modify their work.

> Children need to know that some things will remain the same each day, for example, that the woodworking bench and necessary materials and tools will always be there for them to use; that there will always be some paint; that those favourite books, or a story read today, will be there again to enjoy tomorrow. They need to know that if they begin something today they will be able to complete or add to it tomorrow, thus developing their own continuity of thought and action.
>
> (Nutbrown 1999)

Displays have an important part to play in the creation of a stimulating environment and their role in promoting learning is discussed in chapter 5.

In developing long-term plans for areas of provision, practitioners will be able to ensure that sufficient on-going opportunities are provided across the areas of learning and that the curriculum is balanced. An overview of all the plans will show clearly how each area of learning is developed throughout the setting. The process of long-term planning will help practitioners to focus their own thoughts and ideas and will, if undertaken collaboratively, establish a clear, whole-team approach and commitment to the curriculum. The plans should be regularly reviewed by the team and modified in response to assessments of children's use of, and observed learning in, each area of provision (see pp. 133–136).

Long-term plans should be clearly written and follow a common format. They should be made readily available to any adult involved in supporting children in the learning process and also to adults visiting the setting in a monitoring or inspecting role. They offer a framework for teaching and learning and an explanation of curricular aims.

The depth of planning involved in creating a rich learning environment may not always be understood by visitors, and the 'free flow' system in operation in many settings is sometimes regarded rather dismissively as children 'just playing'. However, as discussed in the Introduction, children learn to make sense of the world around them through play – it is their 'work' and as such should be afforded the high status and considered planning it deserves. It is as a result of thoughtful and informed resourcing and organisation of the environment in which children play that learning experiences of the highest quality consistently take place.

Planning an area of provision should start with the question: what opportunities for learning do we want to offer children? In all areas of provision, there should be planned opportunities for:

- Practising and refining skills
- Acquiring knowledge and developing concepts, and for consolidation
- Developing positive attitudes to learning.

Such opportunities for learning should be identified in plans. Also included in a long-term planning structure for areas of provision will need to be:

- Key areas of learning and pertinent early learning goals
- Resources: permanent, rotated, additional (e.g. to support a particular topic or focus activity); organisation of resources and area
- Anticipated learning experiences and activities; suggested extension or focus activities (see also chapter 2)
- The role of the adult in supporting learning.

Teams of practitioners may decide to adopt a framework for long-term planning recommended by, for example, their LEA, or may devise their own. If the latter decision is taken, practitioners should ensure that all the above points are addressed.

Practitioners may choose to display information, such as a brief explanation of learning intentions and a list of key early learning goals, in each area of provision. Such information can be a useful prompt to adults working with children in the area. It may also give parents and carers a deeper understanding of children's learning, enabling them to support their own child's learning more effectively. (Other ways of communicating information to parents and carers are explored in detail in chapter 4.)

The inside area

Commercially produced resources are numerous and vary enormously in quality and usefulness. Equipment should be selected according to its effectiveness in supporting planned learning and there will probably be a number of alternatives that will be equally successful in facilitating learning. The following example illustrates the variety of resources that could be used to support children on their journey towards a specific goal in a particular area of provision.

CASE STUDY

Area of provision

- Sand

Key area of learning

- Mathematical development

Working towards QCA early learning goal

- Use language such as 'heavier' or 'lighter' to compare two quantities.

Possible resources

- Bags of sand, empty bags (to be filled with sand and compared in weight)
- A range of stones and pebbles (to be compared with each other and against amounts of sand)

- A range of graded plastic cylinders (to be filled with sand and compared in weight)
- A selection of 'junk' containers such as yoghurt pots, margarine pots and plastic bottles (to be filled with sand and compared in weight)
- Four identical containers to be filled with e.g. sand, sawdust, cotton wool or water, and then compared in weight
- Simple balance
- Plank balanced on a narrow wooden block (children attempt to keep the plank horizontal by placing e.g. sand bags of equal weight on each end)

In order to encourage independent learning, resources in areas of provision should be readily available and accessible to children, and should be stored in clearly labelled drawers, boxes or baskets, or on templated open shelving or unit tops (see pp. 12–13).

It is a characteristic of many early years practitioners that they are 'hoarders' and reluctant to throw anything away in case it 'comes in useful'! It is true that such resources often prove to be very valuable in supporting learning and as practical storage equipment and, of course, reduce the strain on limited budgets. The workshop area is usually a very popular area requiring a constant supply of 'junk' materials to feed children's enthusiasm for design and technology and it is a good idea to encourage parents to become hoarders of such materials too! Other examples include the following:

- Large, transparent, plastic 'pop' bottles with the neck and top removed have a wealth of uses e.g. as containers for growing beans, as containers for exploring capacity and volume, as containers for holding water (children mark-making using water and brushes outside). The 'cut-off' tops of bottles can be used as funnels in the sand and water areas.
- Plastic film canisters make useful individual PVA glue containers – their tight-fitting lids ensure that glue remains in good condition.
- Old kitchen equipment can be used for making marks, exploring shape and creating texture in clay (e.g. forks, potato 'mashers', spoons, biscuit cutters, rolling pins), for investigations into the properties of water and sand (e.g. slotted spoons, sieves, tea strainers, colanders) and for imaginative play in the home corner (e.g. baking tins, plastic bowls, wooden spoons).
- Lengths of plastic guttering can be used to build exciting 'waterways' or 'marble runs'.
- Old car tyres can be used for constructional activities by children outside, as numbered 'targets' (for throwing beanbags into), or as part of an obstacle course.
- Large cardboard boxes (e.g. packaging for furniture and large electrical equipment) make exciting 'den' structures.
- Old, disconnected telephones can be used very effectively in the office, home corner and other areas of provision to encourage children to engage in interactive conversation with adults and other children and to express thoughts and ideas verbally.
- Wire frames from old lampshades serve as frameworks for mobiles, for example, to display children's model fish hanging above the water tray.

Practitioners may decide to make resources in order to ensure that they specifically fit their requirements, including props to support story-telling/making, songs and rhymes such as laminated pictures of characters/parts of text and character puppets (very simple card 'cut-out' characters attached to wooden 'lolly' sticks are effective) or postboxes for the office displaying the name of the setting and session times.

Additional or rotated resources should be well organised and catalogued to ensure that all members of staff are aware of what is available and where it is stored. Practitioners may decide to catalogue under areas of learning, areas of provision or topic areas – there is no right or wrong way here, but the method of organisation should be a matter for discussion by the whole team. Systems should be easy to understand and use and storage arrangements should be practical within the setting.

Examples of additional/rotated resources include:

- Story boxes or bags such as *Dear Zoo* by Rod Campbell (the book, letter to the zoo, plastic zoo animals in boxes/containers, 'puppy' soft toy); *Billy's Beetle* by Mick Inkpen (the book, story tape, plastic beetle in a small box, 'Billy' puppet, 'sniffy dog' soft toy)
- Role-play resource boxes containing equipment for e.g. a hospital, a clinic, a Post Office, a travel agent, or a shop
- Mathematical equipment[1] such as capacity jugs/cylinders, length-measuring equipment, balancing/weighing equipment (standard and non-standard), dice, 'spinners' (number, colour, shape, etc.) sorting/matching/counting toys, pattern-making equipment – to be introduced to areas of provision as appropriate
- Boxes of resources that will promote imaginative play in different areas, e.g. in the sand area – to create a desert/jungle environment – imitation plants (garden centres usually supply a wide range), rocks, pebbles and stones, plastic insects, and reptiles (N.B. Pineapple tops make very effective 'palm trees'.)
- Games – lotto, board games, card games, dice games
- Topic resource boxes, e.g. 'Transport' – fiction and non-fiction books, photographs/ models of different modes of transport, road maps, underground maps, train/boat/bus/aeroplane tickets, road signs, equipment for setting up road systems in the outside area.

Some practitioners may be faced with the problem of sharing a hall or room with other groups and this has implications for organisation of the setting. In such a case, much of the equipment will probably have to be stored away at the end of a session and set out again at the beginning of the next session. It is vital, then, that all involved adults are aware of what provision should be offered to children in order to meet curriculum requirements and that a plan is available of how the basic provision should be organised. In drawing up such a plan, it is important to remember that the arrangement of furniture greatly influences the child's learning. Open areas allow children to observe other children working but more enclosed areas can enable them to concentrate for longer periods, leading to extended explorations and investigations.

Developing literacy and numeracy

In a well-planned environment, the development of literacy and numeracy will take place in all areas of provision and will form an integral part of activities. Nigel Hall, in his book *The Emergence of Literacy*, states that:

---

[1] Much of this equipment will probably be included in the basic provision in certain areas, but duplicates and alternatives should be available for children to use in other areas in order to develop particular skills and concepts.

Children should never need to ask if they can engage in purposeful literacy acts. If a classroom provides an environment where the status of literacy is high, where there are powerful demonstrations of literacy and where children can freely engage in literacy, then children will take every opportunity to use their knowledge and abilities to act in a literate way.

(Hall 1987)

The attitudes towards, and commitment to, literacy established during the early years are crucial in the development of children as readers and writers.

Mark-making equipment should be available in all areas of provision,[2] consisting of a range of mark-making tools (pencils, pencil crayons, ball point pens, fibre tip pens, etc.), paper (the use of recording 'frames', shopping lists and memo pads will encourage children to write for a purpose, but plain paper should also be available), folded cards/sticky labels (for children to mark with their name and use to identify work such as models) and clipboards. Practitioners may want to provide two or three extra writing resource boxes in a 'central' area, which children can transport to, and use in, any activity.

Young children should be encouraged to use the equipment purposefully and to make marks to convey meaning. Their achievements as emergent writers and readers should be celebrated and all developmental stages in literacy development recognised and valued by practitioners. The following examples of children's mark-making to communicate meaning show a range of purposes for writing within the early years setting.

CASE STUDIES

'Telephone message' (Figure 1.1)

This message was written as the child (aged 3 years 6 months) played in the office. Pretending to engage in a telephone conversation with her Mum, she made marks in response to imagined contributions from Mum. During this activity, the practitioner scribed the child's talk (* indicates points at which the child made marks on the paper).

'Yes…yes…I'm at nursery! Yes…Yes…*… No…I'm going to the shop, what do you want?…Fish and chips*…Milk*…Grandma is coming for me at nursery*…I'm having my milk now…Bye!'

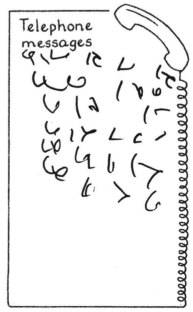

Figure 1.1 Telephone message

---

[2] A wider range of writing equipment will be permanently available in the office area (see p. 22).

'Shopping list' (Figure 1.2)

This shopping list was written by a child (aged 3 years 3 months) during role play in the home corner. He used a circular mark to represent each word on his list and 'read back' the list pointing to a different mark, moving down the page, each time he said a word: 'eggs – bread – chips – carrots – beans – pizza – sausages – apples'. The different marks at the top represent his name. He shows an understanding of features of lists and attempts writing to communicate meaning.

'Lion's visit – building a den: recording frame' (Figure 1.3)

This child (aged 3 years 11 months) spent time building a den for Lion in the construction area. She chose to make a record of her work and completed the 'frame' independently (having previously been shown how to use it). She then showed her work to the adult and gave the following verbal explanation:

Figure 1.2 Shopping list

Name

I built a den for The Lion and his family. This is what the den looks like:

To build the den I used:

cardboard boxes
wooden bricks
paper
material
tape

Figure 1.3 Lion's Visit – building a den: recording frame

'This picture [pointing to the drawing in the top box] is Lion – he is in his den. The leaves are on the top. That [marks to the left of the drawing] is Lion's name.'

When asked what she had used to build the den, she pointed to the marks in the bottom box and said 'boxes, bricks, paper, material, tape'. The child has identified her work by making marks at the top of the page to represent her own name. This example shows that the child knows the difference between writing and drawing and makes that distinction in her own mark-making. She has written to inform, understanding that writing can be read.

'Bear warning!' (Figure 1.4)

This message was written by a child (aged 4 years) to an absent member of staff due to return the next day. The child had been enthusiastically involved in an imaginary 'bear hunt' in the outside play area during the morning. He asked another adult to give his message to the person concerned and offered this explanation:

'We've seen the bear! It's hiding! It's waiting to get us! [Pointing to his mark-making] Dear teacher...there's a bear at nursery!...Don't go outside...the bear will get you! If you want to go out, wait for me and Michael...we know where the bear's cave is!'

The child also drew a picture of the bear (with sharp teeth to show how fierce it was!) – a clear distinction is made between writing and drawing. Marks (writing) are arranged in strings horizontally and display elements of letters (including a recognisable 's' and 'l').

Although it is essential to provide children with a good variety of high-quality fiction and non-fiction books (both in a designated book area and to support learning in other areas of provision), the environment must also offer children a much wider range of reasons and opportunities to read. The presence of bus timetables, recipe cards, magazines in racks and

Figure 1.4 Bear warning

telephone directories in areas of provision will encourage children to incorporate reading into their play (see Figure 1.5). Labels and signs that inform and instruct should be displayed in all areas of the setting, conveying meaning through the written word and through pictures and symbols.

Figure 1.5 Following a recipe to make pasta in the home corner

Cards displayed in areas of provision inviting children to engage in a particular activity serve a dual purpose – to attract interest in the activity and to engage children in reading for a purpose (e.g. 'Would you like to write a party invitation? Who will you invite to the Teddy Bears' Tea Party?' – illustrated with a written invitation and a picture of a bear). It is a good idea to build up a bank of such 'activity cards', which can be repeatedly used. Displaying the cards in moulded, perspex photograph frames will ensure that they are protected from glue, water and paint.

Examples of children's mark-making should be displayed around the setting and their work used, where possible as a resource by other children. For example, plans made by children of their models and constructions, and lists (words or pictures) of components used, can be laminated and displayed[3] in the construction area, or made into books, and used by others to reproduce an identical model (see Figure 1.7, p. 19). Practitioners may decide to scribe young children's verbal explanations/ideas and display them alongside drawings or photographs of models.

Children should have access to cards displaying their names which they can use in their play at any time – to support them when naming a painting or model, or when signing a card or letter, for example. Some children will need to have pictures (probably duplicates of the pictures displayed on their coat pegs) displayed alongside their names as they develop skills of visual discrimination. Children can also use their name cards to register that they are waiting to work in a certain area. By attaching their card to a carpet tile on the wall in the area, or by writing their name on a list, they become 'first in the queue' to work there. When a space becomes available, the practitioner, or other children, will notify the child.

Working towards QCA early learning goals for communication, language and literacy
By the end of the foundation stage, most children will be able to:

- Read a range of familiar and common words and simple sentences independently
- Write their own names such as labels and captions and begin to form simple sentences, sometimes using punctuation.

It is essential that children practise, in order to develop, speaking and listening skills, and these skills are not always given a high profile in planning. It can help to increase adult awareness of the importance of this area of learning and its place in the curriculum by discussing, and highlighting on plans, opportunities for developing speaking and listening skills through activities in areas of provision, as in the following example.

CASE STUDY

Workshop area of provision

Opportunities for development of speaking and listening skills are highlighted in italics.

---

[3] Carpet tiles attached to the wall in each area serve as a good display board – children's work, labels, signs, pictures, posters, poems, rhymes, numbers, plans and instructions will readily 'stick' to the tiles if self-adhesive hook-and-loop fastening tape is applied to the back of each. Resources can be changed quickly and frequently and children are able to move them around on the board. This may not be practical in all settings, in which case portable 'carpet tile' boards (sandwich-board style) can quite easily be made for use in all areas of provision.

Activities/learning experiences

- Making imaginative and functional models using 'junk' materials. *Explaining how the model was made and what materials/equipment was used.* (e.g. Making beds for Goldilocks and the three bears – children could test the beds for strength and then *use them as a prop in their own story-telling*.)
- Making musical instruments to produce a variety of sounds and *comparing children's musical instruments, discriminating between different sounds.*
- Building large-scale models with other children, *discussing plans* and working collaboratively.
- Following written/pictorial plans and instructions, and *following instructions from an audio tape.*
- Exploring properties of materials and *talking about characteristics using descriptive language.*

Working towards QCA early learning goals for communication, language and literacy
By the end of the foundation stage, most children will be able to:

- Enjoy listening to and using spoken and written language, and readily turn to it in their play and learning
- Explore and experiment with sounds, words and texts
- Use language to organise, sequence and clarify thinking, ideas, feelings and events
- Sustain attentive listening, responding to what they have heard by relevant comments, questions or actions
- Interact with others, negotiating plans and activities and taking turns in conversation.

Adults working in the setting should take every opportunity to model literacy skills (e.g. writing shopping lists, passing on telephone messages – written and verbal, writing letters, cards, invitations, writing 'reminder' notes, giving and responding to verbal instructions, following written plans, reading stories and information books) and to work alongside the children, supporting them in the development of writing, reading, speaking and listening skills.

Children's mathematical development arises out of daily experiences in a rich and interesting environment.

(QCA 2000)

It is important that numbers are displayed throughout the setting and accessible to children. Vertical and horizontal 'number lines' should be in evidence and can be presented in a variety of ways, including the following:

- Number train – each carriage numbered 1–10 (the corresponding number of 'lolly stick' puppets can be placed in each carriage, e.g. one rabbit, two frogs)
- Number washing line – children peg numbered clothes onto the washing line in the correct order
- Number ladder attached to the wall – each rung is numbered and children help 'Monkey' (soft toy) to climb the ladder, counting as he steps on the rungs
- Autumn leaves – cardboard or real leaves (these will be preserved if laminated) numbered and hanging from trees outside or hanging from mobiles inside.

A 'bank' of numerals and number lines in each area of provision will encourage children to use numbers in their play.

Story boxes, as well as offering rich opportunities for development of language and literacy skills, can be planned with objectives for numeracy in mind. *Kipper's Toybox* by Mick Inkpen is an ideal story through which to develop counting skills. The provision of a cardboard box containing Kipper's toys and a copy of the book in the book area will inspire children to retell the story counting the animals in and out of the toy box.

The way in which equipment is stored and presented to children can, as well as encouraging independent learning, support the development of mathematical concepts as illustrated in the following example.

CASE STUDY

Water area of provision

Resources

- Three measuring cylinders (a range of sizes)

Organisation

- Children select cylinders from, and return them to, templates of the bases of the cylinders applied to the open shelf in size order. This will encourage discussion of size and use of language such as 'bigger', 'smaller' and 'circle', and of positional language such as 'next to'. 'Upright' templates applied to the back of a shelving unit will also encourage comparison of height and the use of related language (see Figure 1.6). Numbering of the cylinders, 1, 2, 3, and corresponding numbering of templates, will encourage counting with one-to-one correspondence, and matching, naming and ordering of numerals.

Working towards QCA early learning goals for mathematical development

By the end of the foundation stage, most children will be able to:

- Say and use number names in order in familiar contexts
- Count reliably up to ten everyday objects
- Recognise numerals 1–9
- Use language such as 'circle' or 'bigger' to describe the shape and size of solids and flat shapes
- Use everyday words to describe position.

In areas such as the workshop, painting area, malleable materials area and water area, where children are required to wear aprons as they work, the provision of, for example, four numbered aprons in each area serves a few purposes. Numbered aprons hung on numbered hooks will encourage children to match and order numerals 1–4 and to use the number names (e.g. 'I'll use number 1 apron and you have number 2'). The number of children working in an area will be restricted by the number of aprons available (e.g. four aprons: four children) and children will soon begin to use vocabulary involved in addition and subtraction (e.g. 'There are only three children in here – there's one more apron – you can come in, then there will be four').

Figure 1.6
Selecting
equipment in the
water area

Working towards QCA early learning goals for mathematical development
By the end of the foundation stage, most children will be able to:

- Say and use number names in order in familiar contexts
- Count reliably up to ten everyday objects
- Recognise numerals 1–9
- In practical activities and discussion begin to use the vocabulary involved in adding and subtracting.

Sorting resources can be part of the 'tidying-up' routine and to engage children in purposeful activities of this nature practitioners will, again, need to give careful consideration to the storage of resources in areas of provision. Storage containers should be sturdy and clearly labelled with words, symbols and/or pictures. Children will need to be taught how to sort the resources and given an explanation of the criteria used. Practitioners may decide to change the sorting criteria for a particular resource from time to time in order to encourage the development of certain concepts. For example, interlocking plastic bricks can be sorted according to colour, length, shape or purpose.

Long-term plans for areas of provision

This section of the chapter looks in detail at, and gives specific guidance on, long-term planning for children's learning in the following areas of provision:

- Construction
- Water
- Office/mark-making
- Role play (home corner)
- Painting.

Long-term plans are organised under the headings:

- Learning opportunities
- Key areas of learning
- Working towards QCA early learning goals in key areas of learning
- Resources
- Organisation
- Learning experiences/activities
- Adult role
- Key questions
- Vocabulary.

These plans are offered as exemplars. It is hoped that practitioners will be able to adapt them for use in their own settings, and refer to the model when planning other areas of provision.

Where space is abundant and the setting well staffed, it will be possible to offer children a full range of equipment all the time, although staff will undoubtedly decide to plan additional resources to support topic work or focus activities. Other practitioners will need to carefully plan the rotation of resources to ensure that children have constant access to equipment that provides them with intended learning opportunities.

In every well-planned area of provision, valuable learning is likely to take place across the curriculum. Practitioners should always be aware of the numerous and diverse learning experiences possible and take every opportunity to extend children's learning in all areas. However, each area of provision has its own particular strengths in terms of promoting learning in key areas, and these are identified on the exemplar plans. Practitioners may wish to focus on different key areas of learning and this is perfectly acceptable as long as the resources reflect and support the focus, and the curriculum is broad and balanced across the setting as a whole. The goals included in each plan are those on which learning is most clearly focused in the key areas.

There will be a certain amount of repetition from plan to plan and practitioners will note that some goals are evident in a number of different plans. This is inevitable when producing separate and complete plans for each area of provision and only serves to emphasise, once again, how entwined the curriculum is with the environment.

'Organisation' and 'adult role' are other examples of sections in which certain points will be common to a few areas of provision. For the purpose of this book, these 'common points' are listed below, and only points exclusive to the area are included in each plan. However, in practice, it is advisable to produce long-term plans inclusive of all aspects of these sections. This will ensure that every plan is useful in its own right as a support for those adults working with children in that particular area – cross-referencing can be frustrating to the busy practitioner and confusing to the visitor.

Aspects of organisation common to all areas of provision

- Resources easily accessed by children to encourage self-selection and independent learning
- Clear cataloguing of and storage arrangements for rotated/additional resources and a rota/plans for their inclusion in the provision

- Daily checking, and replenishing, of consumable resources (e.g. mark-making equipment)
- Regular focus activities and periods of observation planned
- Key early learning goals displayed in the area
- Children sign list, or engage in a similar activity, to register that they have worked in the area.

Aspects of 'adult role' common to all areas of provision
The adult will:

- Provide good-quality resources and organise the area
- Be aware of the goals in the key areas of learning and the steps taken on the journey towards the goals
- Interact with children, asking questions and making suggestions to support their learning
- Be familiar with key vocabulary – model, and support children in their use of, key words
- Work alongside children, modelling skills and attitudes
- Read with children from fiction/non-fiction books, plans, instruction cards, etc.
- Scribe children's ideas/thoughts and display their work
- Observe children's learning and use of the provision
- Assess children's development/progress.

All long-term plans refer to examples of focus activities sited in that particular area of provision – detailed plans for these activities can be found in other chapters of this book and page references are given for each.

The wide range of children's learning needs within the foundation stage is reflected in the planned provision and suggested learning experiences/activities and resources should enable progress to be made from individual starting points, through the 'stepping stones' towards the key early learning goals.

Construction area

Practitioners will need to provide as large a space as possible as work in the construction area often expands as it develops and frequently involves a number of children working on a 'project'. It may be that two or three children choose to work individually in the area, in which case there will still need to be ample room to avoid frustrations and physical limitations on their work. The area will probably need to be carpeted or a rug provided as children tend to spend most of their time in this area sitting, kneeling or lying on their tummies!

Small-world equipment, although not construction equipment, is included in the 'resources' list. Its use by children in this area often results in the extension of an activity and in the development of language and creativity (e.g. see 'Jungle Play' plans, chapter 3).

Children should be taught to value other children's work and to celebrate achievements. An area for displaying children's models (e.g. a wall shelf, cupboard top, free-standing open shelving unit – see chapter 5, figure 5.6) should be made available and children encouraged to make name cards for display next to their work. Although the display area needs to be in a position where children can look at and talk about each other's work, they should be discouraged from touching or handling the work of others without their permission.

The following plan focuses on construction provision inside the setting – there will also be rich opportunities for construction on a larger scale in the outside play area and a list of appropriate resources can be found later in the chapter (p. 37).

Learning opportunities

- *Skills:* Exploring, building, constructing, assembling, joining, planning, problem solving, evaluating, modifying, adapting, recording, explaining, expressing ideas, observing, comparing, estimating, questioning, selecting and using equipment appropriately, writing/making marks to communicate meaning.
- *Attitudes:* Valuing and showing respect for resources and other children's work, independence, cooperation, interest, enthusiasm, enjoyment, responsibility, concentration, perseverance, confidence.
- *Understanding/knowledge:* Being familiar with the names, characteristics and uses of different construction kits and components, making comparisons (e.g. shape, size, length, colour), measuring length (non-standard), increasing spatial awareness, counting with one-to-one correspondence, developing understanding/use of mathematical language, finding out how to make a strong/balanced structure, using reference books/diagrams/plans to inform own planning and constructing, being aware of design purposes, making up/recreating stories, recreating roles.

Key areas of learning

- Knowledge and understanding of the world (design and technology)
- Mathematical development
- Communication, language and literacy

Working towards QCA early learning goals in key areas of learning

By the end of the foundation stage, most children will be able to:

- Ask questions about why things happen and how things work
- Build and construct with a wide range of objects, selecting appropriate resources, and adapting their work where necessary
- Select the tools and techniques they need to shape, assemble and join the materials they are using

(Knowledge and understanding of the world)

- Count reliably up to ten everyday objects
- Use language such as 'circle' or 'bigger' to describe the shape and size of solids and flat shapes
- Use everyday words to describe position
- Use developing mathematical ideas and methods to solve practical problems

(Mathematical development)

- Enjoy listening to and using spoken and written language, and readily turn to it in their play and learning
- Use language to recreate roles and experiences
- Use talk to organise, sequence and clarify thinking, ideas, feelings and events
- Interact with others, negotiating plans and activities and taking turns in conversation
- Attempt writing for various purposes, using features of different forms such as lists, stories and instructions.

(Communication, language and literacy)

Resources

- Open shelving, templated for e.g. wooden blocks
- Open shelf unit on which to display children's models
- Plastic storage baskets and boxes clearly labelled with equipment names and pictures (e.g. cut out from catalogues)
- Carpet tiles on wall/free-standing board
- A range of appropriate fiction and non-fiction books
- Plans[4] (e.g. architects' plans, 'flat pack' furniture plans), diagrams, instructions, photographs of constructions (e.g. Eiffel Tower, fairground wheels, houses from different cultures) – displayed on wall/board
- Maps – roads, underground
- Examples of e.g. mechanical toys, clock workings
- Large set of wooden 'unit' blocks
- Construction kits (it is better to provide three or four well-stocked sets that will enable children to develop a range of skills than lots of poorly-stocked sets which will lead to frustration) – interlocking bricks, equipment with connectors, cogs and wheels, screws and bolts
- Train track and train
- Small-world people, farm animals, zoo animals, dinosaurs, cars
- Mark-making equipment – plastic carrying basket containing pens; pencils; rulers; small, blank, folded card labels (for children to name their own work); clipboards; plain paper; simple planning 'frames'
- Measuring 'sticks'
- A4 file containing plastic pockets in which children can file their own work to create a central resource of children's plans for use by whole group

Organisation

Aspects exclusive to the construction area are listed here (see pp. 14–15 for 'common aspects'):

- Large, carpeted area to be available.

---

4 Include examples of children's work and photographs.

Learning experiences/activities

- Handling and exploring equipment
- Making models with adult support
- Making own models independently
- Working collaboratively to produce a group model
- Designing and making for a purpose; e.g. make a container for the straws on the milk table (such challenges can be repeated and children asked to use different construction sets)
- Talking about own and others' work, identifying successful areas and suggesting improvements
- Explaining to an adult/other children how a model has been made
- Following instructions (pictorial, written or from an audio tape)
- Giving verbal instructions to an adult/another child
- Looking at non-fiction books/plans and using information to support own work
- Recording own work (sequencing cards, drawings, lists)
- Naming work and signing the area 'register'
- Dismantling models, sorting and counting components and matching resources to templates using mathematical language and correct names
- Using stories/experiences as a stimulus for creative play and small-world equipment to build environments around their models

☞ **Examples of focus activities in this area:** see 'Jungle play' and 'Lion's visit' plans, chapter 3 (pp. 62 and 64).

Adult role

Aspects exclusive to construction area are listed here (see p. 15 for 'common aspects'). The adult will:

- Model skills involved in building and constructing
- Support children in making/reading plans
- Make diagrams and lists showing components used in a child's model (see Figure 1.7).

Key questions

What did you use to make your model? How did you make it? What did you do first? What do you need to make a car? What does the plan tell us? Can you find the parts shown on the plan? What is your model for? Which part do you think works the best? How could we make the tractor move? Will it go faster if we use bigger/smaller/more wheels? Is the garage big enough for the car? How could we make it bigger? What will happen if a car knocks into it – can we make it stronger? Can you build a bridge tall enough for the bus to go under?

Vocabulary

Big(ger), small(er), long(er), short(er), tall(er), circle, square, rectangle, triangle, sphere, cube, cuboid, cone, cylinder, names of component parts, number names (1–10), positional language (e.g. next to, in front of, on, under, behind), directional language (e.g. forwards, backwards)

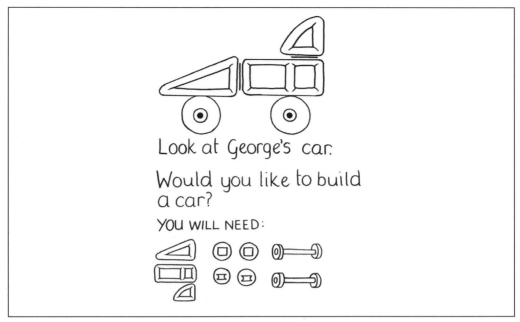

Figure 1.7 George's car – practitioner's drawings of the components used by George in his model will support other children in their attempts to produce an identical car

Water area

The water area needs to be carefully positioned to allow staff easy access to taps and a sink. Some puddles on the floor are inevitable during enthusiastic investigations and surfacing should be 'non-slip'. There should be enough room for children to move freely around the water tray and also for them to construct water ways, siphoning systems, etc. Practitioners may want to restrict the number of children working in the area and, as mentioned earlier in the chapter, provision of a specified number of waterproof aprons is an effective way of limiting the group size. Aprons should be easy for children to put on and take off and should cover as much of their clothing as possible!

A tiled area around the tray is a good idea but not practical in all settings. Storage containers should be waterproof and, ideally, have holes in the base and sides as resources are often put away wet and soon become mouldy if not allowed to dry out properly – plastic baskets are suitable and readily available in many supermarkets and hardware shops.

It is difficult to display books in the water area without risking damage to them although there are some book stands on the market that do offer protection (e.g. perspex cookery-book stands). Laminated blank sheets of paper for use with markers enable children to record without the worry of soaking their paper – these can be displayed on carpet tiles[5] on the wall or on a board, or can be attached to clipboards.

---

[5]   Markers can also be kept on the carpet tile if a strip of self-adhesive hook-and-loop fastening tape is attached to the shaft.

Learning opportunities

- *Skills:* Investigating, experimenting, estimating, comparing, using descriptive/key vocabulary, problem solving, selecting and using equipment appropriately.
- *Attitudes:* Sharing/turn taking, cooperation, collaboration, independence, enthusiasm, curiosity, motivation, concentration, confidence, respect for resources and the work/ideas of others.
- *Understanding/knowledge:* Developing an understanding of: volume, capacity, size, shape, number, displacement, forces (e.g. floating/sinking, siphoning), absorption, dissolving, heating/cooling. Being familiar with/using mathematical language related to these concepts.

Key areas of learning

- Knowledge and understanding of the world (scientific development)
- Mathematical development
- Communication, language and literacy

Working towards QCA early learning goals in key areas of learning

By the end of the foundation stage, most children will be able to:

- Investigate objects and materials by using all of their senses as appropriate
- Find out about, and identify some features of, living things, objects and events they observe
- Look closely at similarities, differences, patterns and change
- Ask questions about why things happen and how things work

(Knowledge and understanding of the world)

- Say and use number names in familiar contexts
- Use language such as 'more' or 'less', 'greater' or 'smaller', 'heavier' or 'lighter', to compare two numbers or quantities
- Use language such as 'circle' or 'bigger' to describe the shape and size of solids and flat shapes
- Use developing mathematical ideas and methods to solve mathematical problems

(Mathematical development)

- Use talk to organise, sequence and clarify thinking, ideas, feelings and events
- Interact with others negotiating plans and activities and taking turns in conversation.

(Communication, language and literacy)

Resources

- Water tray (with differing base levels)
- Water – sometimes coloured (using food colouring)
- Mop and bucket
- Wooden board to fit across the tray (perhaps with an arrangement of pipes fitted through holes drilled in the board)
- Open shelving, templated for e.g. jugs, cylinders
- Plastic storage baskets, labelled
- Four waterproof aprons

- Graded sets of jugs, measuring cylinders, beakers, buckets
- Funnels, sieves, slotted spoons, ladles, water wheels, watering cans, siphons, tubes, pumps
- Natural materials such as sponges, corks, pebbles, pumice stones, shells, driftwood, fir cones, bark
- Transparent plastic bottles (different sizes/same size but marked at different levels with waterproof tape)
- Tea set – cups, teapot, jug, spoons
- A range of small-world creatures, people, boats
- Clipboard, laminated paper, markers
- Posters, photographs, poems (preferably laminated), fiction/non-fiction books

Organisation

Aspects exclusive to the water area are listed here (see pp. 14–15 for 'common aspects'):

- Four children only allowed in the area (to be controlled by the provision of four aprons)
- Resources easily accessed by children, and equipment allowed to drain until dry
- Water tray to be emptied at the end of every session
- Colour to be added to the water as planned (in short-term planning).

Learning experiences/activities

- Observing other children working in the area
- Observing/exploring properties of water
- Pouring from, and filling, containers, counting how many of one fit into another
- Comparing and ordering containers
- Matching equipment to templates
- Investigating and experimenting using appropriate equipment and materials: e.g. displacement – transparent plastic containers, pebbles, coloured water; heating/cooling water – ice blocks (perhaps coloured, or containing objects such as buttons) added to warm water in the tray, snow in the tray
- Discussing ideas with adults and other children
- Making predictions and drawing simple conclusions
- Simple recording – checklists, charts
- Imaginative 'sea world' play
- Using stories as a stimulus for imaginative play

☞ **Examples of focus activities in this area:** see 'Making boats', chapter 2 (p. 53) and 'Investigating snow', chapter 3 (p. 84).

Adult role

Aspects exclusive to the water area are listed here (see p. 15 for 'common aspects'). The adult will:

- Ensure safety at all times (e.g. any excess water on the floor to be mopped up)
- Encourage children to experiment and 'find out'
- Work alongside children experimenting and modelling use of equipment.

Key questions

What do you think will happen if: We pour the water from this container into that one? We tip the jug this way? We lift up this end of the tube while the water is inside? We put a stone into this jug (full of water)? We put the sponge into the water? We squeeze the sponge in the water? Do you think the shell will float? Can you find something that you think will sink? Were you right? Why do you think it sinks? How many jugfuls of water do you think will fit into the bucket? Do you think the jug holds more or less water than the cylinder? How can we make water travel upwards? How can we make the boat move in the water without touching it?

Vocabulary

Full(er), empty, emptier, big(ger), small(er), tall(er), short(er), wide(r), long(er), thin(ner), heavy, heavier, light(er); wet, dry, warm, hot, cold, freeze, melt, pour, flow, float, sink; equipment names

Office/mark-making area

The office area is the obvious place in which to focus on developing learning in the area of communication, language and literacy. Resources should be provided that enable and encourage children to engage in reading, writing and speaking and listening activities for a 'real' purpose.

The area does not require the same amount of floor space as, for example, the construction area, but should be large enough to allow for movement of individuals without disturbance to other children. Many practitioners find that 'enclosing' the office area on two or three sides (using tall shelving units or screens) encourages children to concentrate for longer periods by excluding unnecessary distractions. This structure also reduces the volume of noise in the area, enabling the children to more easily engage in interactive conversation (e.g. using telephones).

Practitioners will need to be permanently looking out for resources to enhance the provision in this area (e.g. old catalogues, telephone directories, obsolete forms, used tickets). The rate at which children use consumable resources, such as paper, in the office is surprisingly fast – it can be quite a challenge to supply according to demand!

The provision of various different papers and formats (e.g. lined, squared, headed writing paper, memo pads) will encourage children to engage in meaningful writing for a range of purposes. Practitioners can easily design these themselves and, if access to a photocopier is available, they should keep a file of master copies to enable them to replenish stocks quickly.

Learning opportunities

- *Skills:* Recording; mark-making (to communicate meaning); using mark-making tools with control; reading (pictures, symbols, words); designing and making; decision making; observing; forming relationships; listening; communicating through talk – explaining, expressing, discussing, negotiating, questioning, requesting.
- *Attitudes:* Independence; enjoyment; motivation; confidence; concentration; cooperation; interest in, and respect for, the ideas and work of others.

- *Understanding/knowledge:* Understanding that meaning can be communicated through writing, and that reading is a way of accessing information from the written word; knowing the basic conventions of written English; developing a knowledge of the sounds and letters used in English; understanding that spoken language can be used to communicate, negotiate and discuss; understanding the importance of listening in an interactive conversation.

Key areas of learning

- Communication, language and literacy
- Personal, social and emotional development

Working towards QCA early learning goals in key areas of learning
By the end of the foundation stage, most children will be able to:

- Enjoy listening to and using spoken and written language, and readily turn to it in their play and learning
- Use talk to organise, sequence and clarify thinking, ideas, feelings and events
- Interact with others, negotiating plans, activities and taking turns in conversation
- Hear and say initial and final sounds in words, and short vowel sounds within words
- Link sounds to letters, naming and sounding the letters of the alphabet
- Read a range of familiar and common words and simple sentences independently
- Know that print carries meaning and, in English, is read from left to right and top to bottom
- Attempt writing for various purposes, using features of different forms such as lists, stories and instructions
- Write their own names and other things such as labels and captions, and begin to form simple sentences, sometimes using punctuation
- Use their phonic knowledge to write simple, regular words and make phonetically plausible attempts at more complex words
- Use a pencil and hold it effectively to form recognisable letters, most of which are correctly formed

(Communication, language and literacy)

- Continue to be interested, excited and motivated to learn
- Maintain attention, concentrate and sit quietly when appropriate
- Have a developing awareness of their own needs, views and feelings and be sensitive to the needs, views and feelings of others
- Form good relationships with adults and peers
- Select and use activities and resources independently.

(Personal, social and emotional development)

Resources

- Round table and four chairs
- Wall space or large, permanent board (possibly covered in carpet tiles for use with self-adhesive hook-and-loop fastening tape[6]) displaying e.g. greetings cards,

---

[6] Children are more likely to use displayed labels and signs in their play if they can remove and transport them to where they are working.

invitations, signs, labels, alphabet, photographs of children writing for different purposes

- Large permanent board (or wall) displaying children's name cards (removable)
- Cork notice board
- Calendar
- Postbox
- Open shelving unit
- Two telephones
- Keyboard
- Bank of 'Can you ring this telephone number ....?' cards
- Telephone directories, catalogues, brochures
- Laminated message board (A4) with marker pen
- Address books, diaries, memo pads
- Bank of word/phrase cards (e.g. 'Happy Birthday', 'with love from', 'to')
- Paper, various sizes: blank, lined, squared, headed paper
- Forms, tickets
- Folded card (for making greetings cards), postcards
- Envelopes, used stamps
- Sticky labels, card labels, tape, glue sticks
- Hole punches, staplers, scissors, sharpeners, rubbers
- Pencils, ball point pens, felt pens, crayons
- Clipboards

Organisation

Aspects exclusive to the office area are listed here (see pp. 14–15 for 'common aspects'):

- Different order forms, letter headings, blank invitations, etc. to be introduced regularly
- Area to be situated in a quiet position away from 'thoroughfares'.

Learning experiences/activities

- Mark-making using a variety of tools
- Writing for a range of purposes, e.g. invitations, letters, orders, greetings cards, postcards, telephone messages, envelopes, memos, lists, forms, diary entries
- Posting/receiving written communications
- Writing own name, e.g. signing letters
- Reading for a range of purposes, e.g. letters/cards/notes/invitations from friends, own writing, catalogues, brochures, telephone numbers
- Discussing work and ideas with adults and other children
- Dialling telephone numbers and holding two-way telephone conversations with adults and other children

☞ **Example of focus activity in this area:** see 'Writing party invitations to teddy bears', chapter 2 (p. 49).

Adult role

Aspects exclusive to the office area are listed here (see p. 15 for 'common aspects'). The adult will:

- Model reading and writing in a variety of situations and for a variety of reasons
- Hold telephone conversations with children in the area
- Ensure that all letters etc. are collected from the postbox daily and distributed to children concerned.

Key questions

Would you like to answer the telephone? Who is it? Why did they ring? Can you take a message? Can you read the message to me? Who would you like to ring up? What is their telephone number? What will you ask/tell them? Can you read your letter to a friend? How do you know who the letter is from? What will you write on the envelope? Which books would you like to order from the book club? Can you find your name card? Which is the first letter in your name? What sound is at the beginning of your name? Can you find the letter 'b'? Can you make a 'b' with your pencil? Would you like to send your friend a birthday card? Can you find her name card? What would you like to write? Can you find the label that says 'Happy Birthday'?

Vocabulary

Children will be expected to understand/ use the following words and types of words: letters, words, numbers, write, read, send, listen, talk, hear. They will also be familiar with: letter and number names (some or all) and vocabulary related to equipment and materials

Role play – the home corner

The home corner is an example of a role-play area. Through role play, children learn about real life and relationships in a 'safe' situation, and can represent experiences and ideas in their play. They can often be observed imitating adults in the context of 'everyday' life, as illustrated in Figure 1.8. A well planned role-play area should also provide rich opportunities for developing communication, language and literacy, offering purposes for writing, reading, speaking and listening.

The possibilities for role play in early years settings are almost infinite but the range and quality of provision is largely dependent on the fertility of the practitioner's imagination! Areas for role play are often constructed as part of a theme, or may be planned in response to a child's, or group of children's, interests.

Listed below are some examples:

- Hospital, doctor's surgery or clinic
- Post Office, bank
- Travel agents
- Supermarket
- Shoe shop

Figure 1.8 Preparing for a shopping trip

- Toy shop
- Hairdressers
- The 'Three Bears' House'
- Aeroplane, bus, train, boat
- Bear cave, lion's den
- Castle
- Hotel, café, restaurant
- Ice cream van
- DIY store
- Library.

In many settings, if space allows, the home corner is part of the permanent provision and additional role-play areas are constructed temporarily in other sites, often in the outside area. Sometimes the home corner may consist of a kitchen with dining and sitting area, sometimes it will have a bedroom. Often a change or rearrangement of furniture will reawaken interest in the home corner, as will a focus activity such as a birthday party, Diwali celebration, or the arrival of a new baby (doll!).

The following long-term plan relates to a home-corner area comprising kitchen and dining/sitting area.

Learning opportunities

- *Skills:* Sharing, taking turns, observing, communicating, imagining, initiating and developing imaginative ideas, recreating roles, story-making.
- *Attitudes:* Respect for self and others, independence, cooperation, caring, social awareness, sensitivity, self-assurance, resourcefulness, enjoyment.
- *Understanding/knowledge:* Extending language; using skills for a real purpose; developing understanding of, and knowledge about, relationships/roles/cultures/ needs of others/purposes of writing, reading and talking; 'real life'/home environment/social 'rules' and codes of behaviour; appropriate expression of feelings.

Key areas of learning

- Personal, social and emotional development
- Communication, language and literacy

Working towards QCA early learning goals in key areas of learning

By the end of the foundation stage, most children will:

- Have a developing awareness of their own needs, views and feelings and be sensitive to the needs, views and feelings of others
- Have a developing respect for their own cultures and beliefs and those of other people
- Respond to significant experiences, showing a range of feelings when appropriate
- Work as part of a group or class, taking turns and sharing fairly, understanding that there need to be agreed values and codes of behaviour for groups of people, including adults and children, to work together harmoniously
- Understand what is right and wrong and why

- Consider the consequences of their words and actions for themselves and others
- Understand that people have different needs, views, cultures and beliefs, which need to be treated with respect
- Understand that they can expect others to treat their needs, views, cultures and beliefs with respect.

(Personal, social and emotional development)

By the end of the foundation stage, most children will be able to:

- Enjoy listening to and using spoken and written language, and readily turn to it in their play and learning
- Use language to imagine and recreate roles and experiences
- Use talk to organise, sequence and clarify thinking, ideas, feelings and events
- Interact with others, negotiating plans and activities and taking turns in conversation
- Attempt writing for various purposes, using features of different forms such as lists, stories and instructions.

(Communication, language and literacy)

Resources

- Home-corner furniture at child height: cupboards, sink, washing machine, table, four chairs, sofa, cooker
- Draining rack, kitchen utensils, trays, chopping boards, saucepans, wok, colander, imitation food
- Cups, saucers, bowls, plates, cutlery (in coloured sets)
- Tea towels, oven gloves, tablecloth
- Recipe cards (see Figure 1.5) and books
- Pegs, washing line, iron, ironing board
- Brush, dustpan, vacuum cleaner
- Open 'wardrobe' storage unit (on castors), coat hangers
- 'Dressing-up' clothes (from a range of cultures)
- Dolls (male, female, ethnic characteristics)
- Baby clothes, blankets, shawls, bath, push-chair
- Mark-making equipment, note pads, shopping lists, paper, notelets, envelopes, invitations, birthday cards
- Telephone, address book, telephone directory
- Magazine rack, containing magazines, catalogues, etc.

Organisation

Aspects exclusive to the home corner are listed here (see pp. 14–15 for 'common aspects'):

- Furniture arranged to create the feeling of a real room
- Enough space allowed for cupboard doors to open easily, and for children to be able to move freely around furniture.

Learning experiences/activities

- 'Playing out' real-life situations and personal experiences
- Fantasy play and story-making

- Dressing-up
- Discussing experiences, ideas and negotiating roles, delivering messages
- Making 'props' for play
- Writing for a purpose (e.g. shopping lists, telephone messages, invitations)
- Celebrating birthdays and festivals

☞ **Example of role-play focus activity:** see 'Post Office role play', chapter 3 (p. 82).

Adult role

Aspects exclusive to the home corner are listed here (see p. 15 for 'common aspects'). The adult will:

- Engage in role play with the children
- Plan additional resources for celebrations.

Key questions

Who would you like to invite for tea? How will you invite him? (telephone? written invitation?) What will you make for tea? What does he like to eat? What do you need to make pizza? Can you find a recipe for pizza in the book? Why is your baby crying? How does she feel? What can you do to make her feel better? What are you going to buy at the shop? What do you need from the shop for your baby? What do you need to take with you to the shop?

Vocabulary

- 'Feelings' vocabulary e.g. happy, sad, cross, angry, worried, frightened
- Vocabulary related to resources e.g. cup, saucer, plate

The painting area

The painting area should, ideally, be situated near to a sink so that children can fill up their own water pots and wash up utensils without leaving too long a paint trail on the floor!

Although ready-mixed paints are appropriate in some circumstances (e.g. printing), children should be offered frequent and regular opportunities to mix their own powder paint, exploring colour blending and a range of consistencies (see Figure 1.9). If children are mixing their own colours, it is not necessary to provide them with a large range, but the primary colours (red, yellow and blue) should be available, as these cannot be mixed using other colours. By mixing two primary colours together, children will be able to produce the secondary colours (orange, purple and green). Blue and red mixed together will make purple, red and yellow produce orange, and blue and yellow make green. The addition of white will produce lighter tints, and black (which should be used sparingly), darker shades.

Children need to be taught routines and use of resources, and will probably need regular reinforcement until they feel confident in the area. Some younger children are much more interested in the process of mixing paint than in the application of paint to paper and should be allowed to pursue this interest.

Easels are very popular in early years settings and allow two children to work in a relatively small space. However, it can be frustrating for children, when using watery paint, if their marks are constantly distorted by 'trickles'. Some activities in this area are much more successful on a horizontal surface and, for obvious practical reasons, tables should be covered in a plastic-coated cloth or newspaper. It is not necessary to provide chairs in the painting area and children will be less restricted in their brush strokes if working from the standing position. Aprons should be provided in a place easily accessible to children.

Learning opportunities

- *Skills:* Experimenting, recording, predicting, decision making, describing, explaining, expressing ideas and opinions, mark-making, designing, imagining, creating.
- *Attitudes:* Interest, motivation, independence, cooperation, perseverance, confidence.
- *Understanding/knowledge:* Developing a knowledge about, and understanding of, the changes that occur when powder paint

Figure 1.9 Mixing colours in the painting area

is mixed with water, and when colours are mixed together; understanding two- and three-dimensional representation and composition; organising colours and shapes to produce an image; increasing knowledge about line, tone, shape, space, pattern, texture and form (i.e. the elements of art); knowing purposes of tools and properties of materials; developing an appreciation of art and artefacts.

Key areas of learning

- Creative development
- Knowledge and understanding of the world

Working towards QCA early learning goals in key areas of learning
By the end of the foundation stage, most children will be able to:

- Explore colour, texture, shape, form and space in two and three dimensions
- Respond in a variety of ways to what they see, hear, smell, touch and feel
- Use their imagination in art and design, music, dance, imaginative and role play and stories
- Express and communicate their ideas, thoughts and feelings by using a widening range of materials, suitable tools, imaginative and role play, movement, designing and making, and a variety of songs and musical instruments

(Creative development)

- Investigate objects and materials by using all of their senses as appropriate
- Find out about, and identify some features of, living things, objects and events they observe
- Look closely at similarities, differences, patterns and change.

(Knowledge and understanding of the world)

Resources

- Large, square table (at a comfortable height for standing to work) covered with a waterproof, self-coloured, cloth ('busy' patterns can be distracting when creating an image)
- Two easels with trays attached
- Trolley: surface templated for water pots, palettes, paint containers; tray storage for brushes (varying thicknesses, round and flat), spatulas, rollers, wooden printing blocks, sponges, a range of 'found objects' for making marks with paint (e.g. cotton reels, washing-up brushes, corks, plastic lids)
- Open-shelved paper cupboard; rectangles of paper of varying size and proportions; textured paper (e.g. woodchip wallpaper cut into rectangles); white and coloured paper
- Drying rack (preferably holding work horizontally to avoid paint dripping)
- White, wooden cube (for displaying objects for observation)
- Reproductions of artists' work
- Powder paint (reds, blues, yellows, white and black), ready-mixed paint, water-based printing inks
- Instructions for paint mixing (see chapter 5, p. 124, 'Mixing paint')
- Pencils (for naming work)
- 'Gallery' displaying the work of children and famous artists

Organisation

Aspects exclusive to the painting area are listed here (see pp. 14–15 for 'common aspects'):

- Limit of four children working in the area
- A range of techniques to be explored, and skills taught, through focus activities.

Learning experiences/activities

- Mixing powder paint with water, mixing colours
- Applying paint to paper, drawing with paint using a range of tools
- Painting from observation and imagination
- Collaborative painting on large sheets of paper
- Printing of various kinds, e.g. with sponges, vegetables, leaves, hands, string, card; on fabric, paper, card, wood; taking mono prints (spread mixed paint on a perspex sheet, draw into the paint with finger, press paper onto the image); making bubble prints (mix washing-up liquid with paint in a tray or bowl, blow with a straw until bubbles reach above the rim, place paper over the bubbles); press printing (draw an image onto a piece of specially produced polystyrene using a pencil or modelling tools, roll on ink or paint, press onto paper)
- Pattern-making (repeat, random)
- Painting own models made in the workshop
- Mixed-media work
- Adding extra 'ingredients' to paint to produce different textures
- Discussing children's work and the nursery art gallery
- Looking at and discussing the work of artists

☞ **Example of focus activity in this area:** see 'Mixing textured paint', chapter 3 (p. 67).

Adult role

Aspects exclusive to the painting area are listed here (see p. 15 for 'common aspects'). The adult will:

- Teach and reinforce routines and colour names
- Model skills and demonstrate techniques.

Key questions

What do you think will happen if you mix red with blue? Which colours did you mix together to make green? Which is your favourite colour? Is this blue lighter or darker than that blue? Which brush will make a thin/thick mark? What do you think will happen if you add more water to your paint? Have you used thick or thin paint? What is your painting about? What do you think this painting is about? What do you like best about this painting? What kind of line/shape have you made?

Vocabulary

- Colour names: red, blue, yellow, orange, purple, green, white, black (other colours if children are ready)
- Descriptive words related to the elements of art, e.g. line: wiggly, straight, wavy, zig-zag; texture: rough, bobbly, lumpy, smooth

The outside area

> Well planned play, both indoors and outdoors, is a key way in which young children learn with enjoyment and challenge.
>
> (QCA 2000)

The outside play area is often described as an area of provision but should not be viewed merely as an additional area, more as an extension of the whole setting in which all other areas of provision can be set up – the 'outside classroom'. The size and features of outside areas vary tremendously from setting to setting and it may be necessary to plan areas of provision in the outside area on a rotational basis. Staffing arrangements also have a bearing on the organisation of this area – it may be impractical to offer children free access to the 'outside classroom' throughout the session, but instead to plan a period when all children and staff go outside or plan for groups of children to work outside with a member/members of staff.

Activities taking place in areas of provision inside can often be extended very successfully outside by introducing different resources. For example, learning about how water travels and how it can be used to move objects can take place inside and outside:

- *Inside:* using tubes, marbles and 'pouring' containers in the water tray. Children pour coloured water into the tube and watch it travel along the tube as they lift up one end, they put a marble in one end of a tube and, keeping the tube reasonably level, use water to 'push' the marble along inside the tube.

- *Outside:* using plastic drainage tubes, pipes and guttering (can be purchased from builders' merchants and are relatively inexpensive), two or three water trays, large buckets and bowls, marbles and balls of different sizes, 'pouring' containers (see Figure 1.10). Children work together on a large scale constructing complex waterways, investigating how water travels on inclines, moving water from a tray at one level to another tray at the same/a different level, and using water to 'push' balls along level guttering and transport them to another tray.

Figure 1.10 Water investigations in the outside area

Working towards QCA early learning goals for knowledge and understanding of the world

By the end of the foundation stage, most children will be able to:

- Investigate objects and materials by using all of their senses as appropriate
- Ask questions about why things happen and how things work.

The outside area also offers opportunities for physical activity and development of gross motor skills, which are largely impossible in the inside environment. It is important to ensure that children are allowed sufficient space in which to run, ride (e.g. bikes and scooters) and climb and that each of these activities is afforded its own designated area. Other activities should encourage the development of throwing/catching skills, balancing, jumping and hopping.

Working towards QCA early learning goals in physical development

By the end of the foundation stage, most children will:

- Move with confidence, imagination and in safety
- Move with control and coordination
- Show awareness of space, of themselves and of others
- Use a range of small and large equipment
- Travel around, under, over and through balancing and climbing equipment.

Exciting investigations of the outside environment can lead to valuable learning taking place, particularly in the area of 'knowledge and understanding of the world'. Practitioners should anticipate such learning experiences and plan an outside area that will provide children with a wealth of opportunities to find out about the natural environment and a range of stimuli that will prompt them to ask questions about the world around them.

It is usually possible, even in the smallest of outside areas, to organise such activities as:

- A 'growth investigation' – a range of flowers and vegetables can be grown from seed in pots, troughs or tyres filled with compost (see Figure 1.11)
- Developing a 'wild area' in which children will be able to observe seasonal changes – a small piece of land planted with grass and wild flower seeds, evergreen shrubs, spring bulbs, plants or shrubs that encourage butterflies (e.g. buddleia)

Figure 1.11 Watering the plants

- A 'minibeast investigation' – introduce a few logs and large stones to the wild area – children will be fascinated by the insect life they discover daily underneath the logs and stones (see Figures 1.12 and 1.13).

Figure 1.12 Searching for centipedes

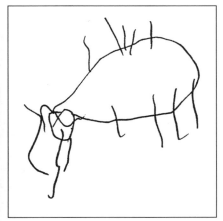

Figure 1.13 Beetle – drawn from observation in the outside area

Working towards QCA early learning goals in knowledge and understanding of the world
By the end of the foundation stage, most children will be able to:

- Find out about, and identify some features of, living things, objects and events they observe
- Look closely at similarities, differences, patterns and change
- Ask questions about why things happen and how things work.

Every effort should be made to promote literacy and numeracy in the outside area. Opportunities for children to practise and develop reading and writing skills are as numerous outside as they are inside but practitioners may decide to select some different resources for use outside. On a dry day, for example, children will welcome the opportunity to make marks, and perhaps write their name, on walls and paving slabs using a paintbrush dipped into a pot of water (see Figure 1.14). Mark-making on a large scale allows children freedom of movement and expression – a roll of decorators' lining paper is inexpensive and, rolled out and secured to the ground with masking tape, provides a 'canvas' large enough for a group of children to work individually or collaboratively with a range of tools. Laminated sheets of A4 card and marker pens can be more practical than paper in wet areas and can also be cleaned and 'recycled'. Portable baskets containing mark-making equipment (including clipboards) are also a useful resource in the outdoor play area.

Figure 1.14 Mark-making with brushes and water in the outside area

Roadways (drawn in chalk on the ground) are always popular with bike riders, and the addition of road signs and arrows encourages purposeful reading. Children will very quickly learn to recognise 'stop' and 'go' on a hand-held sign and to respond appropriately. Other examples of signs that can be displayed outside include 'bus stop', 'taxi rank', 'building site – wear hard hats', maps of the outside play area, shop/garden centre signs, 'follow the trail' arrows, 'are you wearing your outdoor shoes?' Children will often offer their own suggestions and should be encouraged to make and use their own signs.

A bank of illustrated question cards made available to children in the outdoor area will also encourage the development of reading skills: for example, 'Can you find a ladybird?', 'Have you watered the carrots today?' If the pictures are clear and simple, even the youngest of children will be able to 'read' the card and, with support, respond to the questions.

Working towards QCA early learning goals in communication, language and literacy

By the end of the foundation stage, most children will:

- Read a range of familiar and common words and simple sentences independently
- Know that print carries meaning and, in English, is read from left to right and top to bottom
- Attempt writing for various purposes, using features of different forms such as lists, stories and instructions
- Write their own names and other things such as labels and captions and begin to form simple sentences, sometimes using punctuation
- Use their phonic knowledge to write simple regular words and make phonetically plausible attempts at more complex words.

Number plates on wheeled toys, which children match to numbers on 'garages' as they park their vehicles, encourage number recognition, matching and counting. As they become familiar with the system children will begin to refer to bikes by their number – 'It's my turn to play on number three bike now!' – 'Look, "two" bike is still in the garage, you can go on that!' Other ways of developing mathematical learning outside include:

- Hopscotch and grid games painted on the ground
- 'Chant' games such as 'What time is it Mr. Wolf?'
- 'Giant' dice games (roll a 3 – walk three steps across the playground – who will reach the other side first?)
- Playing positional language games, e.g. hide the teddy behind the tree/in front of the den/in the sand tray
- Throwing beanbags into numbered boxes in the correct order (this activity could be presented as e.g. throwing fish to the sealions)
- Making tally charts/tick lists – how many butterflies/cars/people/birds have we seen from the playground during the session?
- Observing insects in 'bug boxes' and counting legs and wings
- Following the 'bear trail' – children step on numbered paw prints to reach the bear's cave
- Posting activities – matching e.g. shapes on envelopes to shapes on postboxes around the area
- Drawing around children's shadows on a sunny day – comparing length and shape
- Measuring children's heights against a wall and making a chalk mark for each child
- Growing sunflowers against a wall – comparing height and recording growth by marking the top of the sunflower in chalk on the wall every week
- Potting plants/planting seeds – comparing different pots – how much compost does this one hold? Does it hold more than that one?
- Fishing for numbered fish in a water tray: using laminated card fish (numbered, and with a metal paper clip attached) and string fishing rods with a small magnet attached – can you catch number one fish? Which number is left in the water?
- Comparing weights / balancing weights – using a rope thrown over a tree branch with a bag full of sand attached to one end, children fill the bag attached to the other end of the rope with sand until the two bags are balanced

- Selecting boxes of suitable size and shape to use as containers for stock in their role-play shoe shop.

All early learning goals for mathematical development are worked towards through this range of activities.

Dens are guaranteed to capture the imagination of young children and the outdoor area is an ideal place in which to set up a bear cave, lions' den, camping holiday tent, teddy bears' hideout or desert island retreat – the possibilities are endless. Wooden structures (e.g. a pyramid) provide a firm framework around which to build a den but if these are not available, large cardboard boxes, tables, etc. can be used effectively. Long lengths of fabric (old curtains or sheets are ideal) draped over the framework instantly create an exciting environment. Other resources can be introduced – the choice of these will depend on the nature of the children's play.

'Shadow play' on a sunny day also offers rich opportunities for creative development, as illustrated in Figure 1.15. Following a story session during which the practitioner read *Where the Wild Things Are* by Maurice Sendak, children experimented with the shadows made by their own body shapes and created some very ferocious-looking 'wild things'!

Figure 1.15 Shadow play: creating 'wild things'

Working towards QCA early learning goals in creative development
By the end of the foundation stage, most children will be able to:

- Use their imagination in art and design, music, dance, imaginative and role play and stories
- Express and communicate their ideas, thoughts and feelings by using a widening range of materials, suitable tools, imaginative and role play, movement, designing and making and a variety of songs and musical instruments.

Opportunities for personal, social and emotional development are many in the outdoor area. Well-planned and exciting activities taking place in this area often play a significant role in motivating children to learn and inspiring in them a desire to explore and investigate the world around them. Children learn to share, and take turns on, equipment and to follow clear codes of behaviour in order to work safely. They develop a responsibility for the care of living things and the environment and are offered opportunities to work independently, in pairs and as part of a group.

To list all the equipment used in the outdoor play area would be to duplicate much of the content of the long-term plans for areas of provision already included in 'The inside area'. For this reason, only examples of resources that are exclusive to the outdoor area are listed below:

- Climbing equipment – frames, ladders, slides (positioned on soft surface)
- Fabric tunnels, plastic 'barrels'
- Wheeled toys – bikes, scooters, 'go-carts'
- Road signs
- Police/traffic warden/lollipop person uniforms
- Large wooden blocks, e.g. hollow blocks, wooden planks
- Large plastic mats, carpet squares
- Old car/bus steering wheels
- Tyres
- Milk crates
- Cones
- Logs, tree 'stumps'
- Bats, racquets and balls
- Beanbags
- Hoops and rubber quoits
- Skipping ropes
- 'Den' frameworks, lengths of fabric
- Lengths of guttering (can be stored on brackets attached to the wall)
- Large water trays, buckets
- Plastic sand tray or permanent, brick-built sand pit
- Shallow builders' tray, old wooden bricks (see Figure 1.16)
- Trowels, spades, rakes
- Hard, builders' hats
- Wheelbarrow
- Watering cans, plant pots, troughs
- Portable mark-making resource baskets
- Plastic water pots, paint brushes and decorators' brushes.

Figure 1.16 Builders at work

☞ **Examples of focus activity plan for the outside area:** 'Going on a Bear Hunt – obstacle course' (chapter 2, p. 59), 'Taking part in a shape trail' (chapter 2, p. 51).

The environment is the mechanism by which the teacher brings the child and different areas of knowledge together.

(Bruce 1997)

Planning focus activities

Children deepen their understanding by playing, talking, observing, planning, questioning, experimenting, testing, repeating, reflecting and responding to adults and to each other. Practitioners need to plan learning experiences of the highest quality, considering both children's needs and achievements and the range of learning experiences which help them make progress. Well planned play is a key way children learn with enjoyment and challenge during the foundation stage.

(QCA 1999)

A focus activity is an activity or experience that is planned in order to achieve particular objectives. Provision is organised in a way that will enable children to develop certain skills, knowledge, concepts and attitudes, and the role of the adult in supporting their learning is clearly defined.

The content of this chapter is organised as follows:

- The planning process (p. 38)
- Deciding on a framework for planning focus activities – what should be included? (p. 39)
- To what extent should focus activities be planned in advance? (p. 40)
- Planning a focus activity (p. 41)
- Examples of focus activity plans (p. 48).

The planning process

Chapters 1, 2 and 3 are primarily concerned with the long-term planning of provision and with the short-term planning of activities and experiences within that planned environment. It is, however, worth explaining and defining the whole planning process before making the leap from long to short term. This 'process' involves three stages, each 'feeding' into the next, as explained in Figure 2.1.

Why plan focus activities?

Reasons for planning a focus activity include:

- To target, and address the specific needs of, individual children/a group of children
- To highlight a particular area of learning and work towards achieving goals in that area
- To extend play initiated by the children and develop individual/group interests (this area will be covered more fully in chapter 3).

LONG-TERM PLANNING

The learning environment is defined in terms of curricular aims, resources, organisation, adult role, and potential learning experiences. Provision across the setting is planned carefully to enable children to access a broad and balanced curriculum (over the six areas of learning) and to ensure learning opportunities for all children. This planning will form a permanent basis (although it should be reviewed regularly) for medium- and short-term planning.

MEDIUM-TERM PLANNING

A 'unit' of learning is planned for a period of time to take place within the learning environment and the curricular framework (duration will vary but is often between three and six weeks). Planning includes focus activities and anticipated experiences linked to e.g. predictable interests (festivals, seasons, outside visits), a curricular focus or a theme. Assessment opportunities, key area(s) of learning, early learning goals, enhancement to provision and intended outcomes for the end of the period are identified. Sometimes medium-term plans are organised into sub-sections (such as a week-by-week breakdown) to aid the process of informing short-term planning.

SHORT-TERM PLANNING

This involves planning in response to individual needs and interests. It also includes activities/experiences selected from the medium-term plan, detailing how these will be put into practice. Short-term planning is usually undertaken on a weekly or daily basis and defines learning objectives, focuses for observation and assessment, targets and support for individuals, resources, key vocabulary, staff responsibilities, practical information (e.g. speech therapy appointments, anticipated timings of story sessions).

Figure 2.1 The planning process

Practitioners may also decide to plan a focus in an area of provision in order:

- To monitor children's use of resources and the effectiveness of an area of provision in achieving aims stated in the long-term plans (see chapter 1)
- To monitor children's progress, assess needs, and record achievements (see chapter 6).

Deciding on a framework for planning focus activities – what should be included?

It is important to bear in mind the purpose of the plan in terms of its use to the educator when deciding on a structure or format. The main questions to ask when determining what to include should be:

- Who will be using the plan?
- How will the plan support practitioners in structuring high-quality learning experiences?

- What information does the practitioner need in order to be well prepared and provide a rich learning environment?
- How will the plan support the adult in challenging children's thinking and extending their learning?

The plan must 'work' for those using it and standard formats may need to be modified to meet the needs of individual practitioners/teams of practitioners. It may be that the plan will be used by parent helpers, students or temporary staff unfamiliar with the setting, as well as by the permanent members of the team. Content may vary according to the setting and the age of the children.

The team need to discuss what to include in their planning structure, and then select or design a 'workable' format that helps practitioners to organise information in a way that is useful to them. Listed below are suggested areas for consideration:

- Focus area(s) of learning – the objectives may be cross-curricular or linked to a particular area of learning
- Learning objectives – these should be included in a prominent place on the plan
- QCA early learning goals – which particular goals will children be working towards during the activity?
- Target group – the activity may be planned to meet individual or group needs, or may be an activity open to all children but with opportunities for differentiation
- Children's prior learning – what knowledge and understanding can they build on?
- Date, time and expected duration
- Introduction, main activity, finishing off – content for each part of the activity presented in a clear sequence
- The role of the adult
- Questions to ask in order to extend children's learning
- Extension activities
- Key vocabulary
- Resources – basic provision/equipment and materials needed to enhance areas of provision
- Opportunities for assessment – what will the adult observe? How will observations be recorded? How will the information be used?
- Evaluation of the activity
- Targets for the future – where do the children go next?

To what extent should focus activities be planned in advance?

When planning children's learning for the next few weeks (see 'medium-term planning', Figure 2.1), practitioners will discuss, as a team, activity ideas linked to objectives and should include these on the medium-term plan. Opportunities for spontaneous learning will also be anticipated in advance. There will, however, be frequent occasions when the practitioner will want to respond to children's immediate interests, enthusiasms and needs and plan a focus activity accordingly. Decisions of this nature will obviously need to be taken 'in progress' and in response to staff evaluation. Weekly plans should be flexible enough to allow adults to plan a focus activity at short notice.

It is not a productive use of time to be rewriting large amounts of information and practitioners should guard against such practice. Medium-term and long-term plans should help to focus and support adults in their short-term planning, but are not concerned with activity details.

Planning a focus activity

What will the children learn?

This is probably the most important question, and should be the first one asked when planning any activity. What we want the children to learn should be the starting point for planning, and the activity a vehicle for the children's learning.

Objectives may target a particular area of learning or be cross-curricular, but should always be clearly defined. Too many objectives become unmanageable; fewer (two or three will often be enough) carefully considered objectives will enable the adult to focus observations and interventions to support the child on their journey towards the intended outcomes. Focus area(s) of learning should be highlighted on the plan, and pertinent early learning goals identified – this will help practitioners to assess children's achievements in terms of national expectations.

Identifying the reason for planning an activity is the first step towards defining objectives. The practitioner may want to target a particular group of children and relate objectives to their needs – a focus activity can be a particularly effective way of addressing the special educational needs of individuals. In order to set objectives at an appropriate level for the targeted children, the practitioner should take into account prior learning and achievements, and consider where the children need to go next.

CASE STUDY

A group of children have spent time over a period of days investigating a range of containers in the water area. They have poured and filled and talked about their observations. For example, Adam, pouring water from a jug – 'Look! It's going – now it's gone! I'm going to put some more in – right up to the top!' Sarah, using a large container full of water to fill a smaller one – 'It won't fit in it's going over the top'. The practitioner decides to build on this experience and extend the children's mathematical learning through a focus activity. The learning objectives are:

- To make comparisons between containers in terms of capacity
- To use mathematical language[1] when talking about their observations.

When the practitioner decides to focus on goals in a particular area of learning, and intends all children to access the activities, learning objectives should reflect the range of needs, and opportunities for differentiation should be stated on the plan. For example, the practitioner may decide to select this goal for communication, language and literacy:

---

[1] Key vocabulary should be identified on the plan, in this case: 'full', 'empty', 'more', 'less'.

By the end of the foundation stage, most children will be able to:

- Retell narratives in the correct sequence, drawing on the language patterns of stories.

Having made the decision to focus on this particular goal, the practitioner will need to look carefully at the learning that needs to take place before the goal is achieved, and at where individuals are on their journey towards achieving the goal. Learning objectives that take into account the range of needs should then be defined and included, for example:

- To listen with interest, and respond, to a story
- To talk, and respond to questions, about events in a story
- To sequence story illustrations and talk about each picture in turn
- To retell, from memory, key events from a story in sequence
- To retell a story showing an understanding of the elements, and using language such as 'once upon a time', 'then', 'next', 'in the end'.

It is important to remember that, although objectives may target certain areas of the curriculum, other learning will take place during the course of the activity – this may or may not be anticipated but should be valued. The purpose of setting objectives is to focus, not restrict, learning.

Once learning objectives have been identified, the nature and content of the activity can be decided.

The activity – what will the children do?

The next step is to plan an activity that will help children to achieve objectives. The activity should capture their interest and should be embedded in a context that is meaningful to them, as outlined in the following example.

Learning objectives

- To select appropriate tools and materials to build and construct
- To retell key events, in sequence, from a familiar story

Activity: Building houses for the Three Little Pigs

To help the adult in structuring the activity, a sequence of elements will probably be identified in the plan. In the case of the 'Three Little Pigs' example, these could include the following.

Introduction

The adult will read the story of *The Three Little Pigs* and encourage the children to discuss reasons why the wolf was able to blow down the first two houses but not the third.

Main activity

Children will construct three houses using straw, sticks and bricks (wooden, or plastic interlocking). They will talk about the story as they work, discussing characters and events.

Finishing off / follow-up

Children will test each construction for strength, using bellows to emulate the wolf's 'blowing'. The houses they have made will be displayed, and resources made available (all week) so that children can revisit, and other children engage in, the activity. Laminated illustrations from *The Three Little Pigs* book will be displayed alongside the houses and children encouraged to sequence these and retell the story to a friend.

Opportunities for differentiation and extension work

These should also be identified on the plan:

- Recording materials used in the construction of the house (tick lists, written lists, pictorial lists)
- Discussing which materials were the most successful and why (in terms of their properties)
- Looking at materials used to build real houses and at architects' designs
- Making a plan of the made house/designing a different house
- Recording (audio tape) instructions for making a house
- Using 'Little Pig' puppets and puppet theatre to reconstruct the story
- Recording (audio tape) children retelling the story.

Where will the activity take place?

This is an important decision and there will often be a number of alternatives to consider. The nature and quality of the children's learning will be determined to a large extent by the environment in which it takes place. Practitioners may choose to site the activity in an existing area of provision (possibly enhanced with additional resources) or may decide to create a new 'area', which will serve as a particularly rich and appropriate setting for the intended learning.

The following example illustrates the diversity of children's writing experience and the influence of the immediate environment on their learning.

Learning objective: To use writing to convey meaning

Table 2.1 The potential for writing in different areas

Example area	Potential writing experiences
Office	Letters, birthday cards, telephone messages (see Figure 2.2), order forms, memos
Home corner	Party invitations, shopping lists, recipes, menus, telephone messages, catalogue orders, recounts, stories
Construction	Plans, lists, traffic signs, instructions
Water	Poems, lists, records of 'findings'
Book area	Stories, book reviews, information

Table 2.1 indicates examples of potential writing experiences in different areas. The choice of area may be influenced by the interests of targeted children. Those children who prefer to spend their time building castles in the construction area may not be inspired to engage in a writing activity in the office. This would be good reason, then, to take the writing to the construction area and ensure that it had meaning for those children. Activities could include: listing the resources they had used to build their castle, writing a story about their castle, writing invitations to the 'Castle Ball' and addressing envelopes to their favourite toys, making signs which direct the guests to the ballroom.

Figure 2.2 Taking a telephone message in the home corner

Alternatively, the adult may want to encourage children to work in an area that they rarely choose to frequent in order to develop certain skills and knowledge. In this case, the nature of the activity needs to have appeal for those children. For example, a group of children who show little enthusiasm for working in the construction area, but who frequently choose to play in the home corner, could be encouraged to engage in a building/constructing activity in the construction area by being challenged to build a table for their teddy bears' picnic, or a bed for their dolls, which they could then transfer to, and use in, the home corner.

Resources – what should be added to basic provision?

The resources offered to the children will be very influential in shaping their learning and should always be of the highest quality. If an activity is sited in a permanent area of provision, it may be that the basic resources in this area are adequate in supporting the specific learning identified in the plan. It will almost certainly be the case that children use basic resources to some extent. Practitioners may decide to 'enhance' provision in an area by adding extra resources in order to attract the children to the activity, stimulate imagination, help them to develop particular skills, knowledge and concepts, and as an extension of the basic provision, as in the following example.

CASE STUDY

Activity: Making musical instruments in the workshop (Figure 2.3)

- *Basic workshop resources:* cardboard tubes, range of plastic tubs and pots, cardboard boxes, plastic bottles, treasury tags, paper clips, paper fasteners, rubber bands, glue (sticks and PVA), glue spreaders, sticky tape, masking tape

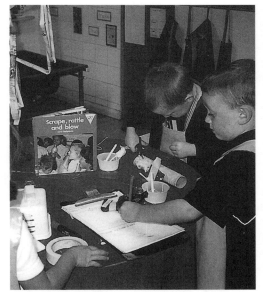

Today I made a musical instrument. It looks like this:

The sound my musical instrument makes is:

loud

quiet

Figure 2.3 Making musical instruments in the workshop area

Figure 2.4 Making a musical instrument – recording frame

- *Additional resources:* a range of musical instruments, tape recorder and a range of taped music; for use in 'shakers': sand, dried peas, beads, buttons, pebbles, dried leaves; for use on 'drums': pieces of fabric, thin plastic sheeting; recording 'frames' (for use by children – see Figure 2.4)

When a temporary area is set up, it will comprise mostly resources additional to basic provision, although some will probably be duplicated in other areas of the setting.

CASE STUDY

Role play: Travel agents

- *Duplicated resources:* pens, pencils, crayons, paper, clipboards, scissors, glue sticks
- *New resources:* travel brochures, booking forms, travel tickets, posters (holiday destinations, modes of transport), travel and transport information books, till, money

Adult role – what will the adult do?

It is important to remind practitioners at this stage of their role as a valuable resource in the context of children's learning. The precise role of the adult will vary according to the activity, but in general terms, it is to support, directly or indirectly, the children's learning. Direct support will involve:

- Stimulating children's interest in an activity
- Providing high-quality resources

- Listening and responding to children's talk
- Questioning children in order to extend learning (questions should be differentiated to address individual needs – see examples of activity plans)
- Working alongside children, modelling skills and use of key vocabulary
- Encouraging, reassuring and praising children
- Valuing and celebrating children's achievements.

A period of observation before intervening in children's play will help the adult to decide on the timing and nature of the support:

> To make certain that positive intervention does not become futile interfering in a child's learning process, it must be preceded by sensitive observation and interaction with the child.
>
> (Nutbrown 1999)

Indirect support includes assessment, which starts with observation of children at work. In some circumstances, observation will be the main role of the adult, but there will be times when balancing interaction with observation seems an almost impossible task. This aspect of the educator's role is explored in greater depth in chapter 6, but, with regard to the focus activity, practitioners may find that referral to the learning objectives on the plan helps them to focus their observations, as in the following example.

CASE STUDY

Learning objectives

- To identify and talk about features of living things
- To use books as a source of information

Activity: observing tadpoles

Observation

Kylie, watching the tadpoles, remarked: 'Look! Their legs are growing – I can see them wriggling when they swim. They haven't got any arms but their tails are very long – their tails are swimming too.' Kylie spent a few minutes studying the tadpoles and then asked: 'When will they go on the rock – when will they jump?' Supported by Mrs Taylor, she found a book about frogs and pointed to a picture of a tadpole, saying 'That's like ours – it's got legs and it's got a tail'. She was interested in looking at the 'frog development' pictures with Mrs Taylor. They discussed what would be the next stage of development for their tadpoles and agreed to watch out for any changes.

Assessment

Kylie shows a keen interest in living things. She is able to recognise and talk about features of living things using everyday language. Kylie understands that information can be found in books. She is able, with support, to read pictures in information books to extend her own learning.

How long should a focus activity last?

The answer to this question is dependent on a number of factors and, although practitioners will need to allocate a 'time slot' on the weekly plan for pre-planned activities, it may be necessary to review timing as the week progresses. For example, children discover a snail in the outside play area on Monday and staff recognise the potential for developing a valuable learning experience. They decide to respond to the children's excitement and fascination by planning time on Tuesday and Wednesday to observe and find out about snails. They postpone the focus activity originally planned for Tuesday to Thursday. In making this decision they are ensuring that both the snail investigation and the planned focus activity receive the adult input, and enthusiasm from the children, that they need to be successful in extending learning.

Practitioners may decide to review the length of time allocated to an activity as they gauge the children's response. It is difficult to anticipate duration and children's interest in the activity is often the deciding factor. Evaluation of the activity as a learning experience may lead staff to develop ideas and plan follow-up activities and extension work. It is often a good idea to make the additional resources used during the activity available for children to access (with or without adult input) for some time afterwards – this allows for exploration of ideas in a less structured context and consolidation of knowledge and concepts. Alternatively, the response of the children may have been disappointing and staff may decide to plan a different activity, but with the same learning objectives. In the latter case, the decision to 'cut short' the activity may be taken – there can be little purpose in pursuing an activity that holds no interest for the children.

How 'rigid' should the plan be?

The activity plan should be seen as a supportive framework within which the practitioner can work to challenge children's thinking and help them to make progress towards achieving intended outcomes. Objectives need to be 'tight' but the plan should be flexible enough to allow for professional judgement – it is the skill of the early years practitioner in recognising when and how to intervene in children's play as it progresses, and the quality of questioning in response to their play, which ensures that children benefit fully from the provision.

What should practitioners consider when evaluating the focus activity?

In order for an activity evaluation to be useful, it must provide practitioners with information that will enable them to improve their practice and focus future planning. This will require consideration of a number of elements and it can be helpful to work within a framework or to use standard 'prompt' questions:

- Children's response – did the activity capture their interest?
- Resources – how successful were they in extending learning? Would staff add/remove any resources if repeating the activity?
- Site of activity – would the activity have been more successful in another area of provision?

- Role of the adult – was the adult able to fulfil the role identified on the plan? Did the adult take on any unexpected roles?
- Children's learning – did the outcomes match the learning objectives? Did any unplanned learning take place – what was the nature of this learning? Was there enough opportunity for differentiation? Have any follow-up/extension activities since been planned?
- What changes, if any, would staff make to the activity? How do they anticipate that these changes would improve the quality of the experience?

Examples of focus activity plans

The following activities are planned in accordance with the guidelines already given in this chapter. Learning objectives focus on a particular area of learning (personal, social and emotional development, communication, language and literacy, mathematical development, knowledge and understanding of the world, physical development or creative development) and one example is given for each area of learning. Chapter 3 also includes examples of focus activity plans, some of which have cross-curricular learning objectives and others objectives that focus on one area of learning. All activities have been 'tested' in an early years setting, have proved successful in achieving objectives and have been received with enthusiasm by children!

The examples of short-term planning for focus activities follow a common format and are organised under the following headings:

- Focus area of learning
- Learning objectives
- QCA early learning goals
- Background information/prior learning
- Introduction
- Main activity
- Finishing off/follow-up
- Adult role
- Key questions/vocabulary
- Resources

Communication, language and literacy: writing party invitations to teddy bears

This activity was planned during a topic on 'bears' and inspired many 'reluctant mark-makers' to attempt writing. It took place during the summer but could be planned at any time during the year. Teddy bears could be invited to festival or birthday celebrations, or to share an indoor 'winter picnic'. The area of provision in which the invitation writing takes place is immaterial as long as adequate and appropriate resources are available to the child, although the most obvious choices are probably the office or the home corner. It is a good idea to inform parents and carers of the focus of the activity so that they can support and extend their child's learning at home – some very polite teddy bears have even been known to reply to the invitations!

FOCUS ACTIVITY:
WRITING PARTY INVITATIONS TO TEDDY BEARS

Focus area of learning

- Communication, language and literacy

Learning objectives

- To understand that print conveys meaning
- To use own writing to communicate meaning
- To practise and develop writing skills in a real context

QCA early learning goals for communication, language and literacy

By the end of the foundation stage, most children will:

- Know that print carries meaning and, in English, is read from left to right and top to bottom
- Attempt writing for various purposes, using features of different forms such as lists, stories and instructions
- Write their own names and other things such as labels and captions and begin to form simple sentences, sometimes using punctuation
- Use a pencil and hold it effectively to form recognisable letters, most of which are correctly formed.

Background information/prior learning

All children will have experience of mark-making with a range of tools. They will be familiar with adults modelling purposeful writing and reading. They will be at different stages in their writing development and the adult will address individual needs in questions asked (adult role, key vocabulary and questions).

Introduction

The adult will show the children an envelope addressed to him/her and ask for suggestions as to what might be inside. A child will be invited to open the envelope and show the contents to the other children. The child will find an invitation inside the envelope – the adult will read the invitation to the children and explain that he/she has been invited to a party by a friend. They will discuss, with reference to the invitation, the purpose, date, time and venue of the party. The adult will suggest that the children hold a picnic party in the outside play area and invite their teddy bears to attend. They will be shown an invitation 'writing frame'.

Main activity

The children and adult will discuss when the picnic/party will take place and all the children will write invitations to their own teddy bears, signing them with their names. The invitations will then be enclosed in envelopes addressed to the bears.

Finishing off/follow-up

The children will take their invitations home to their teddy bears. Preparations will be made for the picnic/party, including shopping lists for food, drinks, paper plates etc.; menus; table labels (children's and bears' names/types of food).

Adult role

The adult will:

- Provide resources
- Stimulate interest in the activity
- Model writing an invitation
- Ask differentiated questions
- Be aware of each child's stage of writing development and support them at that level
- Observe children (re: enthusiasm for mark-making, purposes for writing, pencil control/letter formation) and record observations.

Key questions

What do you think is inside the envelope? Who has sent it? Why? Look at the pictures – do they give us a clue as to what it is about? What do you think the writing says? Where do we start to read the writing? What else do you think might be written on the invitation? Can you see where my friend has written his name? What is your teddy bear's name? Can you write his name on the envelope? Where will you write your name? Can you find your name card and copy your name/write your name without your name card? What else do you need to write on the invitation? Can you read back your writing?

Resources

- Party invitation (written) in envelope addressed to adult
- Invitation-writing frames
- Mark-making tools (pencils, pens)
- Paper, folded card (shopping lists, labels, etc.)

Mathematical development: taking part in a 'shape trail'

The shape trail was planned as part of a focus on mathematical development. Many children had recently shown an interest in using clipboards when mark-making around the setting, and practitioners decided to plan an activity that combined this interest with the learning objectives for mathematical development. The introduction of 'Mr Shape' was intended to stimulate interest in the activity and give children a purpose for engaging in the trail. Because children were required to search the inside and outside areas for shapes, many explored areas that they rarely entered during a 'usual' session. This activity was particularly successful, when children worked in pairs, in terms of peer learning support.

FOCUS ACTIVITY:
TAKING PART IN A 'SHAPE TRAIL'

Focus area of learning

- Mathematical development

Learning objectives

- To match and name regular, flat shapes (circle, triangle, square, rectangle)
- To make records

Extension:

- To make comparisons in relation to size of flat shapes
- To use key vocabulary to describe size

QCA early learning goals for mathematical development

By the end of the foundation stage, most children will:

- Use language such as 'circle' or 'bigger' to describe the shape and size of solids and flat shapes.

Background information/prior learning

Long-term plans for areas of provision include opportunities for children to develop awareness of solid and flat shape and children will have experience of working in these areas. Children will be familiar with the 'flat shape' vocabulary.

Some children will be confident in recognising and naming a circle, square, triangle and rectangle, and will understand the concept of 'big/small' (these children will be targeted for matching two attributes and using flat shape and size vocabulary).

Introduction

The adult will introduce 'Mr Shape' (see resources) and he will show the children some of his shapes (circles, squares, triangles, rectangles). The adult will explain to the children that Mr Shape has lost lots of shapes around the inside and outside play areas. The children will be asked to look for the shapes and record what they find (see resources for differentiation).

Main activity

The children will explore the inside and outside areas looking for Mr Shape's flat shapes. They will work individually or in pairs, talking about what they find and using key vocabulary. Children will record (see resources) the shapes they find.

Finishing off/follow-up

Children will be asked to collect all the flat shapes for Mr Shape and sort them into:

- Circles, squares, triangles, rectangles[2]
- Big/small circles, big/small squares, big/small triangles, big/small rectangles.[2]

[2] Dependent on child's prior learning.

Adult role
The adult will:

- Prepare resources
- Display flat shapes around inside and outside play areas
- Stimulate interest in the activity
- Model use of key vocabulary
- Intervene in children's play as appropriate and support their learning through differentiated questioning
- Observe children re: ability to match flat shapes and use key shape vocabulary/ match two attributes, i.e. shape, size, and use key shape and size vocabulary.

Key vocabulary and questions
Vocabulary: Flat shape – circle, square, triangle, rectangle, shape; Size – big/small, bigger/smaller.
Questions: Can you find a shape the same as this one on your sheet? What is the name of this shape? Can you find another triangle? How many circles have you found? Can you find two more squares? Has Lauren found the same shapes as you? Now you have found a triangle, can you make a mark next to the triangle on your sheet? Is this rectangle bigger/smaller than that one? Can you find a circle that is bigger than this one? How many big triangles have you found and how many small ones?

Resources

- Mr Shape stick puppet (e.g. circular head, triangular legs, square body, rectangular arms)
- Range of flat shapes – circles, triangles, squares and rectangles in two sizes
- Clipboards (one for each participating child), pencils/pens

- Children's recording materials (differentiated):
  - Laminated flat shapes – child will be given one shape and asked to find another to match it (no size differential)
  - Sheet showing one or two shapes – child will mark a mark next to the shape as it is found (no size differential)
  - 'Tick list' showing all four shapes – children make a mark next to a shape every time they see that shape on the 'trail' (no size differential) – see Figure 6.6)
  - Tally charts – children make marks against shapes and count the marks into groups of e.g. five (no size differential).

The adult will introduce the size differential as appropriate and in response to individual needs.

Knowledge and understanding of the world: making boats

This activity was planned following an investigation of materials in the water tray. The practitioner wanted children to use their prior knowledge in responding to a challenge and solving a practical problem. The story *Where the Wild Things Are* was a familiar tale and

Max a favourite character. The story was used to motivate the children, give purpose to their designing, and criteria for success when testing their boat 'structures'. The activity is a good example of using two areas of provision (water and workshop) in one activity, and could take place inside or outside.

FOCUS ACTIVITY: MAKING BOATS

Focus area of learning

- Knowledge and understanding of the world

Learning objectives

- To design and construct for a specific purpose
- To use prior knowledge in problem solving
- To select tools and materials appropriately
- To evaluate the success of a design and make necessary modifications

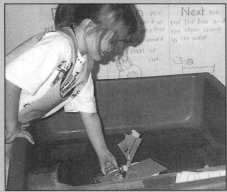

Figure 2.5 Testing Max's boat in the water tray

QCA early learning goals for knowledge and understanding of the world
By the end of the foundation stage, most children will be able to:

- Build and construct with a wide range of objects, selecting appropriate resources, and adapting their work where necessary
- Select the tools and techniques they need to shape, assemble and join the materials they are using.

Background information/prior learning
Children will have been given opportunities for exploration of materials. They will have talked about properties and investigated how different materials react when placed in water. Children will understand the concept of 'floating and sinking' and will be familiar with the key vocabulary. They will have experience of using a range of tools and materials in the workshop area. Children will be familiar with the story *Where the Wild Things Are* by Maurice Sendak.

Introduction
The children will be reminded of the recently read story *Where the Wild Things Are*. The adult will explain to the children that Max's boat has a leak and cannot be used, but that he is desperate to visit the 'Wild Things' again. The adult will show the children models of Max and the Wild Things (Max placed at one end of the water tray and the Wild Things at the other) and ask for suggestions as to how Max could cross the 'ocean'. They will discuss suggestions (see 'key questions') and children will be challenged to build a boat that will carry Max to the 'Wild Things'.

Main activity

The children will build a boat for Max using tools and materials in the workshop (see 'resources'). They will look at information books about boats. They will talk about prior investigations and use their knowledge from these to inform their decisions. They will test their boat in the water tray (see Figure 2.5) to determine whether or not it floats and will make any necessary modifications.

Finishing off/follow-up

Children will put the 'Max' model in their boat and transport him to the other side of the 'ocean' and the Wild Things'. Some children will also record their work (see 'resources').

Adult role

The adult will:

- Provide resources
- Stimulate children's imagination and interest in the activity
- Be aware of children's prior learning and build on their knowledge
- Ask questions in order to extend learning
- Support children in recording their work
- Observe the children re: appropriate use of tools and materials, ability to design for a purpose/evaluate success of their design/modify their design, ability to record work.

Key vocabulary and questions

Vocabulary: Float, sink.

Questions: How can we help Max to cross the 'ocean'? Examples of suggestions might include the following. Make a bridge – how could it stretch all the way across? What could we use to support it? Would it be too far for Max to walk? He could swim – is Max strong enough to swim all that way? How could he carry his suitcase? What would happen if there were sharks in the water? Make a boat – what would we use for the bottom of the boat/the cabin/the sail/the mast? What happens to this material if it gets wet? Do you think this plastic pot will float? Let's test it in the water tray – were you right? How could you stop your boat from sinking? Where will Max sit in your boat? Does your boat still float when it is carrying Max? What did you use to make your boat? Which materials worked/didn't work?

Resources

- *Where the Wild Things Are* by Maurice Sendak
- Max/'Wild Things' models
- Information books about boats
- Basic provision in workshop area and water area (see long-term plans for water area, p. 19)
- Recording frames (e.g. 'My boat looks like this...I used...')

Creative development: story-making/imaginative play

It seems that anything that is introduced to children out of a sealed box, bag or envelope can be exciting to them! Such an introduction, especially when children are encouraged to anticipate what might be inside, is usually very effective in stimulating imagination and inspiring enthusiasm for an activity. In this case, a key inside a decorated box is the stimulus but other resources could be just as successful in prompting creative ideas, for example:

- A tiara in a jewellery box
- A purse in a handbag
- An ornate silver spoon in a velvet pouch
- A photograph (e.g. a character or building) in an envelope
- A gemstone or piece of crystal in a small satin-lined box
- A large, exotic shell wrapped in tissue paper.

Whatever the stimulus, during an activity of this nature the practitioner should provide children with the necessary resources for them to develop their imaginative ideas.

The introduction of this particular activity took place in the book corner. This area was chosen because it was enclosed on three sides (and relatively free from distractions) and because there was ample provision for all involved children to sit comfortably. The story-making and imaginative play took place throughout the setting but, as play progressed and it was agreed that the key probably opened a box of treasure lost at sea, children and staff decided to build a ship in the outside area so that they could search for the treasure.

FOCUS ACTIVITY: STORY-MAKING/IMAGINATIVE PLAY

Focus area of learning

- Creative development

Learning objectives

- To respond imaginatively to a stimulus
- To express thoughts and ideas through imaginative play

QCA early learning goals for creative development

By the end of the foundation stage, most children will be able to:

- Respond in a variety of ways to what they see, hear, smell, touch and feel
- Use their imagination in art and design, music, dance, imaginative and role play and stories
- Express and communicate their ideas, thoughts and feelings by using a widening range of materials, suitable tools, imaginative and role play, designing and making, and a variety of songs and musical instruments.

Background information/prior learning

Children will have experience of listening to stories and of engaging in/observing imaginative play.

Introduction
The adult will show the children a 'very special box' and ask them to guess what is inside. The box will be opened to reveal a key (see 'resources'). Children will be encouraged to handle the key in turn and describe how it looks and feels.

Main activity
The adult will lead the children, through questioning (see 'key questions'), in creating a story around the key. They will express ideas which the adult will scribe. The children will then be encouraged to work as a group to develop their 'key story' ideas through imaginative play. Children will use the key, and other props (see 'resources'), in their play.

Finishing off/follow-up
Children will be encouraged to share their stories and ideas with other children at a group gathering. Some children will record their story ideas pictorially and/or in a written form. A book will be compiled using photographs taken of resources and children's play, and children's story ideas (recorded by them or scribed by the adult). Children will be allowed continued access to resources, and time, to develop ideas.

Adult role
The adult will:

- Provide resources
- Stimulate interest in the activity and build up anticipation (re: opening the box)
- Ask questions, and make suggestions, in order to develop imaginative ideas
- Encourage children to express ideas, and value their contributions
- Scribe children's ideas
- Support children in recording their ideas at their own level
- Observe children's play re: response to activity, use of imagination, ability to express ideas; record observations in individual profiles
- Photograph children at play
- Compile a book of their work.

Key questions
Where do you think the box was found? Who left it there? What do you think is inside the box? Who does the key belong to? What has happened – has the person lost the key? – has it been stolen? What will the key open – a secret door? – a box? – a cupboard? – a treasure chest? – a case? What will you do with the key? Where will you go – how will you use it? How will you find the owner of the key? Who will go with you? What happens on your journey to find the owner of the key?

Resources

- A 'special box' (e.g. painted gold and decorated with 'jewels') containing an elaborate key
- Additional resources such as large cardboard boxes, pieces of fabric, a variety of hats
- Mark-making tools, paper
- Camera

Personal, social and emotional development: showing and talking about special toys from home

The 'special toys' activity was planned during a 'toys' topic but also to address the needs of some of the newer or less-sure children in the setting. Staff had recognised that group discussions were often dominated by the more confident children and that some individuals were not participating at all. They planned an activity that would offer each child an opportunity to contribute without competition, and encourage all children to listen to, and value, the contributions of others.

Children are likely to feel more confident when talking about personal experiences, familiar situations and their own belongings, and some of the children's responses to the 'special toys' activity surprised even the staff. Supported by an adult, and with their own toy as a 'prop', children who usually took a passive role during group discussions were suddenly forthcoming, responding enthusiastically to questions and giving full demonstrations to the group of, for example, the capabilities of their remote-control cars or the musical ability of their singing teddy bears! The 'Special Toy Book' of photographs proved to be very popular and prompted much discussion between children.

FOCUS ACTIVITY: SHOWING AND TALKING ABOUT SPECIAL TOYS FROM HOME

Focus area of learning

- Personal, social and emotional development

Learning objectives

- To share experiences and feelings in a familiar group
- To speak confidently when it is their turn
- To listen to, and value, the contributions of others

QCA early learning goals for personal, social and emotional development

By the end of the foundation year, most children will:

- Be confident to try new activities, initiate ideas and speak in a familiar group
- Maintain attention, concentrate, and sit quietly when appropriate
- Have a developing awareness of their own needs, views and feelings and be sensitive to the needs, views and feelings of others
- Work as part of a group or class, taking turns and sharing fairly, understanding that there need to be agreed values and codes of behaviour for groups of people, including adults and children, to work together harmoniously.

Background information/prior learning

Attitudes of respect for the feelings of others and interest in the experiences and work of others are promoted through all areas of provision and learning. Children will be familiar with the following 'rule': sit quietly and listen when it is someone else's turn to speak. A letter of explanation about this activity will have been sent home and parents/carers encouraged to discuss with their child: choice of toy, reasons for choice, feelings about the toy, history of/experiences with the toy.

Introduction

The adult will invite the small group of children to bring their special toys and join her/him in a comfortable area of the setting. The children will be asked to sit in a circle.

Main activity

The adult will show the children a toy from her/his childhood and explain why the toy holds special memories. Individual children will be encouraged to talk about their own special toy and other children will be given opportunities to ask them questions. When all the children have had a turn, they will sing (to the tune of 'Here we go round the Mulberry Bush'):

> Jack showed us his car today, car today, car today,
> Jack showed us his car today – thank you Jack

This song will be repeated for every child.

Finishing off/follow-up

Children's toys will be kept on the 'special toys display' until the end of the session. Photographs will be taken of each child with their toy and their comments about the toy scribed by the adult. These will be displayed in a 'Special Toy Book' to be kept in the book corner. (N.B. All children will be given the opportunity to take part in this activity over the course of two – three weeks.)

Adult role

The adult will:

- Help the children to feel relaxed in a comfortable and welcoming environment
- Encourage the children to talk about their toys, asking questions and showing interest in what they say
- Remind children of the 'rule' (see 'background information/prior learning') when necessary
- Take photographs of children, scribe their comments and compile the book
- Observe children re: confidence in speaking in a group, ability to use language to express themselves, response to other children's contributions.

Key questions

What have you brought to show us today? Why did you choose this toy to show us? What is special about the toy? What would you like to tell us about the toy? Who gave you the toy? Where/what do you like to play with the toy?

Resources

- Letter to parents/carers to be sent home prior to activity (see 'background information/prior learning')
- Adult's toy
- Children's toys
- Camera

Physical development: going on a 'bear hunt' – obstacle course

This is another example of a favourite story being used as the starting point for an activity (chapter 3 offers further examples of stories as starting points). The 'bear hunt' took place in the outside area and this is the ideal site for the activity. A large hall could be used as a 'wet weather' alternative but, if the hall is not accessible on a permanent basis, use of the resources over the following few days (as recommended in the plan) may be difficult to organise.

The activity allowed staff to observe a range of skills, enabling them to make clear assessments of children's physical development. Most children chose to participate in the activity and some continued to set up their own bear hunts long after the 'focus' had passed.

FOCUS ACTIVITY:
GOING ON A 'BEAR HUNT' – OBSTACLE COURSE

Focus area of learning

- Physical development

Learning objectives

- To develop jumping, balancing, climbing, hopping and running skills
- To move with imagination and confidence
- To develop spatial awareness

QCA early learning goals for physical development
By the end of the foundation stage, most children will be able to:

- Move with confidence, imagination and in safety
- Move with control and coordination
- Show awareness of space, of themselves and of others.

Background information/prior learning
Children will have had daily opportunities to develop gross motor skills. There will be children at different stages of physical development – the activity will be open to all children and the adult should be aware of the range and nature of needs in order to give effective support.

Introduction
The adult will read the story *We're Going on a Bear Hunt* by Michael Rosen, and the children will join in with the words and actions. The adult will ask the children if they would like to go on a bear hunt. They will pack imaginary bags and begin their hunt.

Main activity
The children, with the adult, will follow the obstacle course to the bear cave. This could involve activities such as:

- Climbing over a mountain – climbing up a ladder and over the climbing frame
- Going through a dark tunnel – crawling through the barrel
- Walking over a bridge – balancing on a plank
- Wading through a muddy swamp – walking over tyres
- Crossing a river on stepping stones – stepping on different-sized hollow wooden blocks
- Following a narrow path – walking on a wavy chalk line
- Walking through a thick forest – weaving in and out of cones
- Jumping over a stream – jumping over two parallel chalk lines.

Children may want to chant the words from the *Bear Hunt* story or make up their own chants. When they reach the bear cave, they will go inside, discover the imaginary bear and run to the other side of the play area.

Finishing off/follow-up

The 'bear hunt' obstacle course will be set up in the outside play area for a few days to allow children to revisit the activity and practise skills. The resources may be organised in a different way each day, or new resources introduced, in order to add interest or extend learning.

Adult role

The adult will:

- Set up obstacle course and bear cave in outside play area
- Read the story and stimulate interest in the activity
- Lead the 'bear hunt'
- Encourage children to join in
- Talk to them using suggested vocabulary
- Support children at their own stage of physical development
- Observe children re: physical skills, confidence, spatial awareness, and record their achievements.

Key vocabulary and questions

Vocabulary: The adult will use, and encourage the children to use, words such as 'through', 'over', 'under', 'in', 'out', 'up', 'down'.

Questions: Can you go over/under the bridge? How will you get to the other side of the river? Is there enough room for you and Tom to be on the bridge at the same time? Can you step across the stream or do you need to jump? Can you walk in between the cones without touching them? Can you step from the middle of one tyre to the next without touching the rubber? Can you balance on the top of the tyre?

Resources

- *We're Going on a Bear Hunt* by Michael Rosen
- Tyres, wooden planks and blocks, barrel, ladders, climbing frame, cones, chalk

The valuing and sharing of children's play by adults can only serve to increase the status of the activity and the self esteem of the child.

(Abbott and Rodger 1994)

CHAPTER 3

Starting points for developing learning through focus activities

By the end of the foundation stage, most children will:

- Continue to be interested, excited and motivated to learn.

(QCA 1999)

The content of this chapter is organised as follows:

- Planning from children's interests and enthusiasms (p. 62)
- Stories and nursery rhymes as starting points (p. 68)
- Starting from works of art and music (p. 77)
- Visitors and outside visits (p. 81)
- Responding to the weather (p. 83).

Chapter 2 looked at why and how to plan a focus activity, this chapter aims to explore different stimuli for developing learning through focus activities in the early years environment. It consists mostly of ideas and plans that are offered as examples of starting points for activities and are intended to be of practical use to the reader. The list is by no means exhaustive, merely a sample. Early years practitioners are on a constant quest for new and exciting ways of inspiring young children's learning and the pooling of ideas and resources can be a very fruitful exercise. Practitioners may choose to use these plans in a variety of ways – they may follow the plans closely, decide to modify them according to setting and children's needs, or use them as a 'springboard' for their own ideas. Some plans focus learning objectives in one area of learning, others have broader intentions; all follow the same format as the focus activities in chapter 2.

It is a privilege to work with young children for whom learning is an exciting voyage of discovery, and also a great responsibility, since experiences in the early years play a vital part in shaping future attitudes to learning and in inspiring a continuing thirst for knowledge. It is the role of the early years practitioner to nurture and respond to children's natural curiosity and motivation and to engage them in the learning process.

An effective early years curriculum recognises the need for children to be 'active learners'. Through interacting with, and responding to, the world around them, children acquire skills and knowledge and develop concepts. Well-planned provision in the early years environment will offer them a wealth of exciting opportunities for exploration and investigation (see chapters 1 and 5).

Planning from children's interests and enthusiasms

The QCA *Early Learning Goals* (1999) acknowledged the 'provision for children to take part in activities that build on and extend their interests' as good early years practice. A young child's world is their 'classroom'. A great deal of their learning takes place outside the nursery or preschool setting and this should be recognised by the practitioner. Interests and experiences that children bring from home should be valued, celebrated and, if appropriate, used as a starting point for developing learning in the early years setting. Children also develop interests within the setting and may even be inspired by another child's interests, becoming involved in related activities – this situation offers rich opportunities for the sharing of knowledge and ideas and can lead to valuable learning experiences across the curriculum.

CASE STUDY

Joe visited a safari park at the weekend and returned to nursery on Monday full of enthusiasm for the experience. He was given an opportunity to talk about his visit to a small group of children and to show the brochure and plastic elephant he had brought back. Other children were encouraged to ask him questions and a child was asked to bring the box of 'jungle animals' from the construction area. They looked at each animal in turn, naming them and discussing their features. Joe, and the other children, were encouraged to share knowledge and to use information books to further their knowledge.

A group of children (including Joe), inspired by the discussion, went to the construction area and spent the rest of the session building 'jungle environments' and story-making. The adult observed parts of their play and decided to plan a focus in the construction area the next day (see Focus activity: 'Jungle Play').

FOCUS ACTIVITY: 'JUNGLE PLAY' (see Figure 6.5)

Focus areas of learning

- Creative development
- Communication, language and literacy
- Personal, social and emotional development

Learning objectives

- To use resources imaginatively
- To take part as a speaker and a listener in a small group
- To express thoughts and story ideas
- To negotiate and work cooperatively

QCA early learning goals for focus areas of learning

By the end of the foundation stage, most children will:

- Use their imagination in art and design, music, dance, imaginative and role play and stories
- Express and communicate their ideas, thoughts and feelings by using a widening range of materials, suitable tools, imaginative and role play, movement, designing and making and a variety of songs and musical instruments
- Use language to imagine and recreate roles and experiences

- Interact with others, negotiating plans and activities and taking turns in conversation
- Continue to be interested, excited and motivated to learn.

Background information/prior learning

Joe visited a safari park at the weekend. He enthusiastically shared his experiences with a small group of children and has inspired some imaginative 'jungle play' and story-making in the construction area. After observation of children's play, staff agreed that adding extra resources (see 'resources') to the area and planning some adult focus time would be likely to extend their learning in the focus areas.

Targeted group: Joe, Lucy, Sameena, Jake and Andrew (this group will not be exclusive if other children choose to participate in the activity).

Introduction

The adult will show the children the extra resources and explain the purpose of these (i.e. for use by children in their 'jungle play').

Main activity (construction area)

Children will continue their 'jungle play' and story-making using basic provision in the construction area and additional resources (see Figure 6.5, p. 141).

Finishing off/follow-up

Additional resources and the children's constructions will remain in the area to allow for revisiting of the activity and continuation of imaginative play and story-making. The precise nature of any follow-up work will be determined by the direction taken by the children in their play. There may be possibilities for making information or story books using photographs of the children's play, their ideas scribed by the adult and examples of their drawings/writing.

Adult role

The adult will:

- Value children's experiences outside the setting
- Provide resources
- Recognise when to intervene in children's play and when to 'stand back'
- Scribe children's imaginative and story ideas
- Question children about their play
- Observe children re: response to activity, ability to work cooperatively and express ideas, use of imagination in play
- Make book/display (e.g. children's ideas, photographs of their play).

Key vocabulary and questions

Vocabulary: Animal names, e.g. elephant, lion, giraffe, gorilla, crocodile.
Questions: How many different animals live in your jungle? Can you name the animals? Why has this lion climbed to the top of the mountain? Would you like to explain to Lisa why the snake is hiding under the leaves? Are there any people in the jungle? Why are they there? How did they get there? Would you like to go to this jungle? What can you feel/see/hear in the jungle?

Resources

- Basic resources in the construction area including box of 'jungle animals'
- Additional resources: fiction and non-fiction books – about jungles/animals, pieces of fabric (different textures, natural colours), crepe and tissue paper, cellophane, cardboard tubes and boxes

The children's interest in the 'jungle' theme deepened. They revisited the construction area over the course of a few days, modifying their 'jungles' and creating more elaborate and imaginative stories. By this time other children were showing an interest in their work, some attempting to join in and others choosing to observe.

At this point the practitioner decided to plan another focus activity in order to develop particular skills using the jungle interest as a starting point. This time the whole group was involved as a letter from 'Lion' was read out.

FOCUS ACTIVITY: 'LION'S VISIT' (BUILDING A DEN)

Focus areas of learning

- Knowledge and understanding of the world

Learning objectives

- To explore properties of materials
- To select and use tools and materials appropriately
- To design and construct for a specific purpose
- To make plans and list the materials they have used

Figure 3.1 Lion arrives in his box

QCA early learning goals for focus areas of learning

By the end of the foundation stage, most children will be able to:

- Build and construct with a wide range of objects, selecting appropriate resources, and adapting their work where necessary
- Select the tools and techniques they need to shape, assemble and join the materials they are using.

Background information/prior learning

A group of children have been pursuing a 'jungle interest' in the construction area. The focus activity planned in response to this interest has been successful in achieving its objectives and children are still very enthusiastic about the jungle theme. Staff have therefore decided to use the theme again, this time as a starting point for developing technology skills. This activity will be open to all children.

Introduction

The children will be shown a large, 'camouflaged' cardboard box and invited to guess who is inside. 'Lion' will then appear from inside his box (Figure 3.1) and 'tell' the children that he has come to spend some time with them. He will present them with a letter (see 'resources') asking them to build a den for him and his family. Lion will explain to the children that he has brought a box of additional resources with him to help them in this task.

Main activity (workshop/construction area/outside play area)

Children will handle and talk about the resources in Lion's box. They will then use basic provision and Lion's additional resources to build a den to Lion's specifications (see Figures 3.4 and 3.5). This activity can take place in any suitable area (see suggestions above). They will be encouraged to make plans and lists as they work.

Finishing off/follow-up

Children will talk about the dens they have built, explaining what they did and what they used. They will test the dens according to the criteria in Lion's letter: i.e. size, safety and warmth.

Adult role

The adult will:

- Make Lion's box and provide all other resources
- Stimulate interest in the activity, building up excitement during the introduction
- Work alongside children asking questions, modelling (building, drawing plans, writing lists), scribing children's ideas (lists, plans)
- Observe children re: response to activity, appropriate selection/use of tools/materials, imaginative ideas, ability to record ideas.

Key questions

Who do you think is inside the box? Where has he come from? How did he get here? What will you use to build the walls of the den? How can we make the walls stronger? How can we make/support the roof? Is the den wide/tall enough for Lion and his family? How can we make it wider/taller? How can we make the den warmer? What shall we use to cover the floor? What did we use to build our den?

Resources

- Lion (soft toy) inside a box camouflaged with paper/paint/material
- Lion's letter (see Figure 3.2)
- Lion's box of additional resources e.g. cardboard boxes, lengths of fabric, paper (crepe, tissue, etc.), balsa wood, scissors, string, masking tape
- Photographs of lions/jungle environments, maps of Africa, safari travel brochures
- Paper, pens, pencils
- Recording frame (see Figure 1.3, p. 8)
- Outside resources: milk crates, large cardboard boxes, tyres, hollow wooden blocks, planks, lengths of fabric, 'den' frame
- Outside equipment 'tick list' (see Figure 3.3)

Dear Children,

Thank you for welcoming me to your nursery. Your teachers have told me about the exciting jungles you have created in your construction area and I was wondering if you would build a den for my family and me to stay in during our visit.

The den would need to be big enough for 3 cubs, their mother and me. It would also need to be warm and safe.

Can you help?

Yours hopefully,
The Lion.

Figure 3.2 Lion's letter

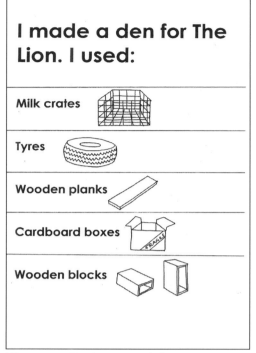

I made a den for The Lion. I used:

Milk crates

Tyres

Wooden planks

Cardboard boxes

Wooden blocks

Figure 3.3 Equipment tick list

Figure 3.4 Lion's den in the construction area

Figure 3.5 Lion's den in the outside area

Sometimes children's interests are of a more investigative nature. The following activity was planned in response to a child's fascination with the consistency and texture of substances such as wet and dry glue, paint and cornflour 'gloop' (a mixture of cornflour and water which changes consistency as it dries out, and which provides compelling tactile experiences!). It is one of many activities that could have been planned to allow the child further scope for exploration.

FOCUS ACTIVITY:
MIXING TEXTURED PAINT

Focus areas of learning

- Creative development
- Knowledge and understanding of the world

Learning objectives

- To explore texture and consistency in paint
- To investigate a range of materials

QCA early learning goals for focus areas of learning

By the end of the foundation stage, most children will be able to:

- Explore colour, texture, shape, form and space in two and three dimensions
- Respond in a variety of ways to what they see, hear, smell, touch and feel
- Investigate objects and materials by using all of their senses as appropriate
- Look closely at similarities, differences, patterns and change.

Background information/prior learning

Staff have noticed Simon showing a keen interest in texture and consistency. All children have experience of paint mixing.

Introduction

The adult will arrange resources on the 'paint table' and encourage children to touch and talk about the dry materials (e.g. sand, sawdust). She/he will then explain that they are going to mix some paint, add different materials to it and then use the paint as a medium to create an image on paper.

Main activity

Children will mix powder paint with water and then choose 'ingredients' to add. They will observe and talk about the changes that occur and compare 'mixtures'. They will then apply the paint to paper and discuss effects.

Finishing off/follow-up

Children's work will be allowed to dry and any changes during the drying process discussed. Their paintings will be displayed in the 'Gallery' alongside original paintings by artists (examples will be selected to show the use of textures, e.g. thick, oil paint).

Adult role

The adult will:

- Provide resources
- Ask questions and encourage use of descriptive vocabulary
- Model use of descriptive vocabulary
- Observe children re: response to activity, expression of ideas and observations, use of descriptive language
- Construct 'Gallery' display.

Key vocabulary and questions

Vocabulary: Children will be encouraged to use descriptive vocabulary related to texture and consistency, e.g. 'runny', 'thick', 'lumpy', 'smooth', 'sticky'.

Questions: What does it feel/look like? Is it difficult to stir? What do you think will happen if we add some more sand? What has happened to the sawdust now you have put it in the paint? How has it changed? Does it pour/drip/fall off your brush? Does it look/feel any different now that it has dried?

Resources

- Powder paint, water, plastic pots, brushes (a range of thicknesses)
- Paper: smooth and textured (e.g. 'woodchip' wallpaper)
- A range of 'ingredients' (e.g. sand, sawdust, PVA glue, rice, soil, flour, cold-water paste (check that it is safe for use by children))
- Original oil paintings

Although an individual child's interest inspired this activity, it was popular with many. Staff were interested to observe that, while most children were keen to apply the paint to paper with brushes, the targeted child was more interested in mixing and stirring and only used the paper as a surface on which to 'drip' the paint mixture.

Stories and nursery rhymes as starting points

Stories are a frequently used starting point for developing learning across all areas of the curriculum and examples have already been cited in chapter 2. Sometimes practitioners will choose a familiar and favourite story or a well-known story character as the stimulus, but in other circumstances may decide that a new story would be more successful in exciting the children. Of course, even though key learning objectives may be focused on an area of learning other than communication, language and literacy, using a story book in this context will help to foster a love of books and to develop skills involved in learning to read.

There is a wealth of beautifully illustrated children's literature on the market that provides practitioners with an almost infinite source of inspiration. A few ideas are given in Table 3.1.

The following 'bridge-building' activity was planned after staff had noticed that, although the large construction equipment was available to children outside on a daily basis, they were not using it very purposefully. The aim was to give children a purpose for design and construction, and the *Billy Goats Gruff* story, as well as being a group favourite, offered a real purpose.

The activity should take place in the outside area if possible. Children will need plenty of space to manipulate equipment and time to test and modify structures. If a large group of children is keen to engage in the activity, it is a good idea to provide a long 'river' so that a number of bridges can be constructed.

Table 3.1 Starting from a story: activities and goals

STORY	POSSIBLE ACTIVITIES	MOST APPLICABLE EARLY LEARNING GOALS
Handa's Surprise by Eileen Browne	• Circle time: being kind to friends • Making a 'carrier' for fruit • Tasting exotic fruits • Writing letters to Handa • Looking at features of our environment and comparing it with Handa's environment	• Have a developing awareness of their own needs, views and feelings and be sensitive to the needs, views and feelings of others • Build and construct with a wide range of objects, selecting appropriate resources and adapting their work where necessary • Investigate objects and materials using all of their senses as appropriate • Attempt writing for various purposes, using features of different forms such as lists, stories and instructions • Observe, find out about, and identify features in the place they live and the natural world
Titch by Pat Hutchins	• Talk about own growth and development from babyhood, remember significant experiences • Measuring height (see p. 72 for activity plan)	• Find out about past and present events in their own lives, and in those of their families and other people they know • Use language such as 'more' or 'less', 'greater' or 'smaller', 'heavier' or 'lighter', to compare two numbers or quantities
Brown Bear, Brown Bear, What Do You See? by Bill Martin Jnr	• Playing with rhyme: anticipating the next animal, substituting own animals e.g. 'I see a pink rabbit looking at me'	• Listen with enjoyment and respond to stories, songs and other music, rhymes and poems and make up their own stories, songs, rhymes and poems
Owl Babies by Martin Waddell	• Talking about nocturnal animals and features of night and day • Exploring a dark den with torches • Circle time: 'Settling in' – helping new children to feel secure and happy in the setting	• Find out about, and identify some features of, living things, objects and events they observe • Ask questions about why things happen and how things work • Have a developing awareness of their own needs, views and feelings and be sensitive to the needs, views and feelings of others
Rosie's Walk by Pat Hutchins	• Setting up a 'Rosie's Walk' obstacle course around the outside area • Looking at how flour is made, and using flour in baking • Making maps and plans: route to the park, plans of the outside area	• Move with control and coordination • Look closely at similarities, differences, patterns and change • Find out about their environment, and talk about those features they like and dislike

Table 3.1 cont

STORY	POSSIBLE ACTIVITIES	MOST APPLICABLE EARLY LEARNING GOALS
Where the Wild Things Are by Maurice Sendak	• Role play – sailing to see the 'Wild Things' • Drawing/painting/making collages of wild things • Making up monster poems/chants • Floating/sinking investigations • Making boats (see p. 53 for activity plan)	• Use their imagination in art and design, music, dance, imaginative and role play and stories • Explore and experiment with sounds, words and texts • Investigate objects and materials using all of their senses as appropriate • Build and construct with a wide range of objects, selecting appropriate resources, and adapting their work where necessary
The Billy Goats Gruff (traditional)	• Sorting and ordering toy goats according to size • Building bridges (see p. 71 for activity plan) • Making goat and troll puppets • Puppet show/role play	• Use language such as 'circle' or 'bigger' to describe the shape and size of solids and flat shapes • Build and construct with a wide range of objects, selecting appropriate resources, and adapting their work where necessary • Use their imagination in art and design, music, dance, imaginative and role play and stories
Kipper's Toybox by Mick Inkpen	• Counting toys in and out of the toy box • Making 'Sock Thing' puppets • Looking at toys from other times	• Count reliably up to ten everyday objects • Select tools and techniques they need to shape, assemble and join the materials they are using • Find out about past and present events in their own lives, and in those of their families and other people they know
The Very Hungry Caterpillar by Eric Carle	• Looking at the life cycle of a butterfly • Looking at colours and patterns on a butterfly's wings and make 'butterfly' prints or collages • Counting the pieces of fruit eaten by the caterpillar	• Find out about, and identify some features of, living things, objects and events they observe • Explore colour, texture, shape, form and space in two and three dimensions • Count reliably up to ten everyday objects

FOCUS ACTIVITY:
BUILDING A BRIDGE FOR THE BILLY GOATS GRUFF

Focus areas of learning

- Knowledge and understanding of the world
- Mathematical development

Learning objectives

- To solve problems and to build for a specific purpose
- To use key mathematical language (see 'key vocabulary and questions')

QCA early learning goals for focus areas of learning

By the end of the foundation stage, most children will be able to:

- Build and construct with a wide range of objects, selecting appropriate resources, and adapting their work where necessary
- Use language such as 'more' or 'less', 'greater' or 'smaller', 'heavier' or 'lighter', to compare two numbers or quantities
- Use developing mathematical ideas and methods to solve practical problems.

Background information/prior learning

Most children will understand the concept of big/small. Some children will have been introduced to the concept of heavy/light. All children will have experience of working with the resources used in this activity. All children will be familiar with the story *The Billy Goats Gruff*.

Introduction

The adult will read the story of *The Billy Goats Gruff* to the children, encouraging them to join in where appropriate; e.g. 'Who's that trip-trapping over my bridge?'

Main activity

The adult, with the help of the children, will create a 'river' and 'fields' using lengths of fabric. Using wooden blocks, planks, etc. (see 'resources'), the children will then work together to construct a bridge(s) over the river.

Finishing off/follow-up

The children will, with adult support, talk about their bridges, considering, for example, successful features, resources used, modifications made (see also 'key questions'). They will use the river, fields and bridges in their play, recreating *The Billy Goats Gruff* story and making up stories of their own.

Adult role

The adult will:

- Provide resources
- Read the story and stimulate interest in the main activity

- Model use of key vocabulary
- Be aware of children's prior learning
- Intervene in children's play as appropriate, asking questions in order to extend learning
- Observe children re: response to activity, use of key vocabulary, understanding of concepts, ability to problem solve, use of resources.

Key questions and vocabulary

Vocabulary:[3] Big/bigger, small/smaller, middle-sized, heavy/heavier, light/lighter, under, on, over.

Questions: Who do you think is under the bridge? Where does the troll live? Who will go over the bridge next? Why does the goat want to go over the bridge? Who is on the bridge now? Which goat is bigger/smaller than the middle-sized Billy Goat Gruff? Which do you think is heavier than the small Billy Goat Gruff? Is your bridge strong enough to support the goats? How could you make it stronger? Is your bridge tall enough for the troll to live underneath? What have you used to build your bridge? Have you used the same resources as William?

Resources

- Story book – *The Billy Goats Gruff*
- Long lengths of fabric (e.g. blue/silver/grey/white for the river, green/yellow for the fields)
- Construction resources: wooden 'hollow' blocks, wooden planks, milk crates, tyres

Involving a popular story character, such as Titch, in activities is a sure way to interest children and to enthuse them for learning. This 'Titch' activity was a variation on the height chart frequently used in early years classrooms to introduce the idea of height measurement. In this case, although all children did record their own height, the main focus was to compare their height with that of Titch using the vocabulary 'tall/taller' and 'short/shorter'. The activity was planned at 'medium-term' stage, as part of a focus on 'mathematical development'.

FOCUS ACTIVITY: ARE YOU TALLER THAN TITCH?

Focus areas of learning

- Communication, language and literacy
- Mathematical development

---

[3] Some children will be ready for using comparative vocabulary. Other children will need more experience of using e.g. 'big/small' but will benefit from adults and peers modelling the use of comparative vocabulary.

Learning objectives

- To listen and respond to a story
- To understand the concept of height
- To use key 'height' vocabulary
- To make simple records and compare findings

QCA early learning goals for focus areas of learning

By the end of the foundation stage, most children will be able to:

- Listen with enjoyment and respond to stories, songs and other music, rhymes and poems and make up their own stories, songs, rhymes and poems
- Use language such as 'more' or 'less', 'greater' or 'smaller', 'heavier' or 'lighter', to compare two numbers or quantities.

Introduction

The adult will read the story of *Titch* to the children using the key 'height' vocabulary.

Main activity

The adult will choose a child of 'average' height to draw around on a large piece of paper. Children will draw clothes and a face on the outline and name it 'Titch'. The adult will attach the drawing to the wall and children will measure themselves against Titch. They each mark their own height on the paper and write their name. They will 'read' their mark and say whether they were taller or shorter than Titch.

Finishing off/follow-up

The children will look at the height chart as a group and count how many children were taller/shorter/the same height as Titch. The Titch height chart will be displayed in an accessible place for children to revisit and discuss. Children will be encouraged to measure themselves against their friends and objects around (e.g. the cupboard, the slide) and to use the words 'taller' and 'shorter' in comparison. A selection of rectangular wooden bricks will be templated vertically against the wall in height order to encourage measurement and comparison.

Adult role

The adult will:

- Provide resources
- Read the story and explain the activity
- Support children in measuring/marking height
- Question children and model use of key vocabulary
- Observe children re: response to activity, understanding of height concept, use of key vocabulary.

Key vocabulary and questions

Vocabulary: Tall/taller, short/shorter.

Questions: Is Titch's brother taller than Titch? Is your brother taller than you? Are you taller than your friend? Can you find anyone who is the same height as you? Do you think you will be taller/shorter than our Titch on the wall? Were you right? Is Titch taller/shorter than you? Look at our chart – how many people are taller/shorter than Titch?

Resources

- *Titch* by Pat Hutchins
- Large sheet of paper
- Pens, pencils

Rhymes can also provide varied starting points for learning across the curriculum and some examples are listed in Table 3.2. The development of rhyming skills is important in the process of becoming a competent reader and repetition of familiar rhymes during an activity will increase children's 'rhyme awareness'. The humour found in many of the traditional and modern nursery rhymes is very attractive to most children — making up new rhymes can be a hilarious experience for them and can become quite compulsive!

FOCUS ACTIVITY: PLAYING WITH RHYME

Focus area of learning

- Communication, language and literacy

Learning objectives

- To listen attentively
- To enjoy and respond to nursery and other rhymes, and rhyming songs
- To show an awareness of rhyme/offer contributions of rhyming words

QCA early learning goals for focus area of learning

By the end of the foundation stage, most children will be able to:

- Listen with enjoyment and respond to stories, songs and other music, rhymes and poems and make up their own stories, songs, rhymes and poems.

Introduction

The children and adult will say some of their favourite nursery rhymes, and sing rhyming songs, together. The adult will invite children to play percussion instruments in accompaniment. They will listen for, and identify, the rhyming words.

Table 3.2 Starting from a nursery rhyme: activities and goals

NURSERY RHYME	POSSIBLE ACTIVITIES	MOST APPLICABLE EARLY LEARNING GOALS
Humpty Dumpty	• Building a strong wall for Humpty Dumpty • Looking at brick patterns	• Build and construct using a wide range of objects, selecting appropriate resources, and adapting their work where necessary • Talk about, recognise and recreate simple patterns
Jack and Jill	• Finding ways of pulling/pushing objects up a 'hill', rolling objects down a 'hill'	• Ask questions about why things happen and how things work
London Bridge is Falling down	• Looking at different bridge structures • Building bridges for different purposes	• Ask questions about why things happen and how things work • Build and construct with a wide range of objects, selecting appropriate resources, and adapting their work where necessary
Baa Baa Black Sheep	• Counting 1–2–3 • Looking at properties of wool, use wool for collage, weaving, sewing, threading, etc. • Weighing/balancing bags	• Count reliably up to ten everyday objects • Investigate objects and materials using all of their senses as appropriate • Use language such as 'more' or 'less', 'greater' or 'smaller', 'heavier' or 'lighter', to compare two numbers or quantities
Incy Wincy Spider	• Looking at, and drawing, spiders and their webs using magnifying glasses • Counting spiders' legs	• Find out about, and identify some features of, living things, objects and events they observe • Count reliably up to ten everyday objects

Main activity

The adult will introduce some new, humorous versions of traditional nursery rhymes, such as:

> Twinkle, twinkle, chocolate bar
> Your Dad drives a rusty car
> Press the starter
> Pull the choke
> Off he goes in a cloud of smoke
> > (Taken from: Foster, J. (1991) *Twinkle Twinkle Chocolate Bar.*
> > Oxford: Oxford University Press.)

> Humpty Dumpty sat on a chair
> While the barber cut his hair
> Cut it long
> Cut it short
> Cut it with a knife and fork
> > (Taken from: Rosen, M. and Steele, S. (1993) *Inky Pinky Ponky.*
> > London: Picture Lions.)

The children and adult will try to think of some versions of their own – the adult will encourage children by making suggestions and asking children for contributions of words to complete the rhyme, e.g.:

> Humpty Dumpty sat on a log
> Humpty Dumpty saw a _____

Children and adult will make up other rhymes, perhaps using the children's names, e.g.:

> Josh is sitting on a chair
> Kate is eating a juicy_____
> Tom is standing on his head
> Liam is sleeping in his_____

The adult will scribe the children's ideas.

Finishing off/follow-up

The children's rhymes will be displayed on the wall and a book of children's rhymes will be compiled. Involved children will be encouraged to share their rhymes with other children. A note of explanation will be sent home with examples of the children's rhymes and parents/carers encouraged to make up rhymes with their children at home. Other poems, rhymes and stories with rhyming words in the text will be read to the children during the course of the week (see 'resources').

Adult role

The adult will:

- Provide resources including a range of rhymes
- Read new rhymes to the children

- Encourage children to make rhyming connections by giving examples and through repetition and emphasis of rhyming words
- Reassure and praise the children
- Display children's rhymes/make rhyme book
- Observe children re: enjoyment of /interest in activity, awareness of rhyme, contributions to new versions of nursery rhymes.

Key vocabulary and questions
Vocabulary: The word 'rhyme' will be used by the adult
Questions: Can you hear the word that rhymes with 'wall'? Can you think of another word that rhymes with 'wall/fall'? Listen to these words, can you add any more? – dog, bog, jog, fog, _____ . Can you read our new rhyme?

Resources

- Books (rhymes, stories, poems): e.g. *Round and Round the Garden* (by Sarah Williams), *Each Peach Pear Plum* (by Janet and Allan Ahlberg), *Hairy Maclary* (by Lynley Dodd), *There's a Wocket in my Pocket* (by Dr Seuss), *All Join In* (by Quentin Blake), *Dragon Poems* (by John Foster and Korky Paul), *Machine Poems* (collected by Jill Bennett)
- Large sheets of paper, pens

Starting from works of art and music

Reproductions of artists' work, original works of art and artefacts from the present and other times, and from different cultures, can provide a stimulating starting point for learning across all areas. In using such stimuli, practitioners are giving children opportunities to become familiar with a selected work of art, or the work of a particular artist, and encouraging them as 'consumers' of art. Visits to art galleries can be very enriching and exciting experiences for young children, but if these are not practical, galleries and museums often offer a 'loan service'.

'Belvedere' by M. C. Escher is a particularly good starting point for 'story-making' by children of all ages.

FOCUS ACTIVITY:
STORY-MAKING/IMAGINATIVE PLAY

Focus areas of learning

- Creative development
- Communication, language and literacy

Learning objectives

- To respond to an artist's work
- To talk about observations
- To use language and imaginative role play to express ideas
- To show an understanding of the elements of stories

QCA early learning goals for focus areas of learning

By the end of the foundation stage, most children will be able to:

- Respond in a variety of ways to what they see, hear, smell, touch and feel
- Use their imagination in art and design, music, dance, imaginative and role play and stories
- Express and communicate their ideas, thoughts and feelings by using a widening range of materials, suitable tools, imaginative and role play, movement, designing and making, and a variety of songs and musical instruments
- Use language to imagine and recreate roles and experiences
- Show an understanding of the elements of stories, such as main character, sequence of events, and openings, and how information can be found in non-fiction texts to answer questions about where, who, why and how.

Background information/prior learning

Children will have experience of expressing ideas through role play and circle-time activities. They will be familiar with looking at, and talking about, works of art (see long-term plans for areas of provision: painting, chapter 1, p. 30).

Introduction

The adult will explain to the children that he/she has brought a very special and exciting picture to show them (the reproduction will be displayed on a board but initially covered by a curtain). The adult will invite suggestions from the children as to what the picture might be about. The picture will then be revealed – 'Belvedere' by M. C. Escher (see Figure 3.6).

Main activity

This will take place with a small group of children. The adult will ask questions about the picture (see 'key questions') and encourage the children to share their observations. On a large piece of paper, the adult will scribe the children's ideas and together they will make up a story[4] about the characters and the building depicted.

Finishing off/follow-up

Children will be encouraged to use 'Belvedere' ideas in their play (additional resources will be provided as required to support play). The children involved in the story-making activity will share their ideas with the rest of the group. The picture and stories will be displayed for all children to look at and talk about, and a 'Belvedere' story book using children's ideas will be compiled by the adult.

---

[4] Children could make up their own stories and use pictures/writing to record their stories.

Adult role

The adult will:

- Provide all resources
- Question children and encourage them to express their ideas
- Scribe children's ideas
- Join in children's imaginative play as appropriate
- Observe children re: use of imagination, ability to express ideas, understanding of elements of stories
- Display picture and children's work/ make "Belvedere" book.

Figure 3.6 Revealing the work of art

Key questions

Where do you think the building is? What are these people doing in the building? Who are they? Where do you think the door at the bottom of the building leads to? Where is the key to the door? Find the man behind the barred window – why is he there? What is he saying? What is the woman at the top of the building looking at? What can she see? Who is the man on the bench? What is he making? What will he use it for? Look at the man and the woman climbing the stairs – what are they talking about? Would you like to go to the building? Who would you go with? How would you get there?

Resources

- A reproduction of 'Belvedere' by M. C. Escher (included in 'Taschen' poster pack: M. C. Escher)
- Large board and 'curtain'
- Large piece of paper, pens
- Additional resources (role-play props) as required

Similarly, listening to music can be a powerful stimulus, particularly in terms of creative and language work. There are many commercially produced tapes and CDs that are suitable for use with children (e.g. instrumental 'mood' music, classical collections) but it is often a good idea to produce a compilation tape with which practitioners feel comfortable, and which will be tailored to fit intentions.

For example, after talking about *The Snowman* story (by Raymond Briggs) with children, the adult may decide to plan an activity with a creative focus. She/he would then select appropriate pieces of music for each part of the story and encourage children to respond to the music through dance and movement. The music chosen to relate to James and the Snowman flying through the air would be a calm and serene piece, whereas the party music would be lively, loud and with a 'dance beat'.

Figure 3.3 Music as a stimulus: activities and goals

STIMULUS	POSSIBLE ACTIVITIES	MOST APPLICABLE EARLY LEARNING GOALS
Listening and responding to music	• Movement and dance using e.g. ribbons, scarves • Expressing feelings: how does this music make you feel? Is it happy/sad/angry music? Listen to the sad music, look in the mirror – can you make a sad face? • 'Painting to music': making marks to match the mood of the music (e.g. large swirling patterns, stamping footprints, splatter painting, angular zig-zag patterns)	• Use their imagination in art and design, music, dance, imaginative and role play and stories • Respond in a variety of ways to what they see, hear, smell, touch and feel • Express and communicate their ideas, thoughts and feelings by using a widening range of materials, suitable tools, imaginative and role play, movement, designing and making, and a variety of songs and musical instruments
Looking at/ listening to musical instruments	• Discriminating between instruments/matching sounds to instruments • Looking at/handling/playing/drawing instruments from own and other cultures • Looking at how musical instruments are made/making own instruments • 'Sound' word poems (listening to different instruments) e.g. 'Tinkling, ringing triangles, Booming, banging drums'	• Recognise and explore how sounds can be changed, sing simple songs from memory, recognise repeated sounds and sound patterns and match movements to music • Begin to know about their own cultures and beliefs and those of other people • Ask questions about why things happen and how things work • Explore and experiment with sounds, words and texts
Making music	• Using musical instruments (own and commercially produced) to accompany own singing/dancing • Exploring rhythm: counting beats, clapping names, playing simple rhythms on an instrument, marching to music/songs • Composing own tunes/sound strings and using a simple system of notation (e.g. based on colour or shape) to record own music • Perform own music to an audience • Record own music on audio tape	• Recognise and explore how sounds can be changed, sing simple songs from memory, recognise repeated sounds and sound patterns and match movements to music • Express and communicate their thoughts and feelings by using a widening range of materials, suitable tools, imaginative and role play, movement, designing and making, and a variety of songs and musical instruments

Working towards QCA early learning goal for creative development

By the end of the foundation stage, most children will be able to:

- Use their imagination in art and design, music, dance, imaginative and role play and stories.

Looking at musical instruments, and making their own music, can also inspire children's learning across a range of curricular areas, as illustrated in Table 3.3.

Visitors and outside visits

Outside visits, and visitors to the setting, offer a host of opportunities for planning exciting learning experiences. Practitioners may choose to link visits to a topic, or plan them with a particular area of learning in mind. Whatever the original intentions, adults should be prepared for unplanned 'spin-off' activities as enthused children direct their own learning – of course, a focus on such activities can be planned at short notice.

Outside visits do not have to be sophisticated, or involve weeks of organisation. A simple walk around the local area can provide the starting point for a range of learning experiences and activities (see Table 3.4).

Table 3.4 A walk around the local area: activities and goals

POSSIBLE ACTIVITIES	MOST APPLICABLE EARLY LEARNING GOALS
• Looking at different buildings/shops, using knowledge in role play in the setting • Looking at numbers/words in the environment (door numbers, street signs), making signs for the setting • Discussing and drawing 'landmarks' and features of the area, making plans of an area/route maps • Counting how many buses go past the park, making tally charts • Observing seasonal changes, bringing back e.g. autumn leaves for observational drawing/further investigation	• Use language to imagine and recreate roles and experiences • Recognise numerals 1–9 • Read a range of familiar and common words and simple sentences independently • Observe, find out about, and identify features in the place they live and the natural world • Count reliably up to ten everyday objects • Find out about, and identify some features of, living things, objects and events they observe

The following role-play activity was inspired by the visit of a Post Office worker known to many of the children as their local postman.

FOCUS ACTIVITY:
POST OFFICE ROLE PLAY

Focus area of learning

- Communication, language and literacy

Learning objectives

- To develop an understanding of the role of the Post Office
- To use knowledge of the Post Office in role play
- To use writing as a means of communication.

QCA early learning goals for focus area of learning

By the end of the foundation stage, most children will be able to:

- Use language to recreate roles and experiences
- Know that print carries meaning and, in English, is read from left to right and top to bottom
- Attempt writing for various purposes, using features of different forms such as lists, stories and instructions.

Background information/prior learning

Children will have experience of writing for a variety of purposes. Children will be at different stages in their writing development – the adult will be aware of each child's prior achievements.

Introduction

The Post Office worker will visit the setting and explain to the children how the Post Office works – the service it offers the community, the different roles of the people who work there, the journey of a letter, and so on. She/he will show the children the uniform worn and equipment used when delivering post. Children will be encouraged to ask questions.

Main activity

Children will:

- Work in the Post Office role-play area, e.g. filling in forms, selling stamps and stationery, stamping passbooks and handling money
- Write letters to friends, family, etc., address envelopes and post letters
- Collect letters from post boxes
- Read labels and signs (see 'resources').

Finishing off/follow-up

Before the children go home, a child will be invited to deliver the post (with adult support). Children will take home letters written to them and to their family members. The Post Office role-play area will be available for children for as long as they show an enthusiasm for working in the area.

Adult role

The adult will:

- Arrange the Post Office worker's visit and prepare the children for the visit
- Support children in asking questions during the introduction
- Provide role-play resources and ensure that the area is well stocked at all times
- Intervene in children's play as and when appropriate
- Ask questions in order to be aware of the extent of children's knowledge and to extend their learning
- Observe children re: purposes for writing, progress in writing development, use of language in role play.

Key vocabulary and questions

Vocabulary: Children will be familiar with 'Post Office' vocabulary, e.g. 'stamp', 'letter', 'envelope', 'address', 'postbox'.

Questions to visitor: What is the job of people who work behind the counter? Where do you deliver post? How many houses do you deliver to? Which streets do you deliver to? What happens to a letter after we put it in the post box? Where does it go before it reaches its destination? Why do people go to the Post Office? How do you help them?

Questions to children: Who are you writing to? Why are you writing to them – what would you like to tell/ask them? Would you like to send a birthday card to Simon? Where do they live? Can you write their name on the envelope? Do you need to go and buy a stamp? Look at the Post Office signs – where can you buy a stamp? How much does it cost? Do you need some money from your Post Office account? Can you fill in a form? Where do you write your name?

Resources

In addition to the Post Office worker, the following will be needed in the Post Office role-play area:

- An area of the setting with furniture arranged to provide a counter, a writing surface and a sitting area (where children can look at leaflets, read letters, etc.)
- Tills, money, stamps, forms (for different purposes), leaflets
- Writing paper, notelets, postcards, greetings cards, envelopes, pens, pencils
- Signs (words/pictures/words and pictures), e.g. 'Buy your stamps here', 'Money bank', 'Postbox – times of collection: 11.00 am/3.00 pm', 'Open/closed', children's name cards
- Fiction/non-fiction books about the Post Office/letters (e.g. *The Jolly Postman* by Janet and Allan Ahlberg)

For another example of an activity involving a visitor, see 'Eeyore's visit to nursery', (Figure 4.1, p. 91).

Responding to the weather

The weather in Britain is characteristically unreliable and most practitioners will know the frustration of planning a paddling-pool activity during a heatwave, only to wake up on the morning of the planned activity to torrential rain! This makes the task of 'timetabling' focus activities related to weather, or seasonal changes, almost impossible. Practitioners should be prepared to respond to weather conditions as they occur, although possible learning experiences and activities can be anticipated in advance.

The arrival of snow is invariably greeted with great glee by children but is not always predicted and rarely lasts for more than a day or two. In the event of a snowfall, the practitioner will probably want to put other plans on hold and take full advantage of the opportunities offered by the 'snow experience'. It is a good idea then, to be prepared with ideas for developing learning and the following plan suggests ways in which children can learn about 'freezing' and 'melting' using snow as a starting point.

FOCUS ACTIVITY: INVESTIGATING SNOW

Focus areas of learning

- Knowledge and understanding of the world
- Communication, language and literacy

Learning objectives

- To investigate the characteristics and properties of snow
- To understand that water freezes and ice melts in response to changes in temperature
- To talk about their observations using key vocabulary

QCA early learning goals in focus areas of learning

By the end of the foundation stage, most children will be able to:

- Investigate objects and materials by using all of their senses as appropriate
- Look closely at similarities, differences, patterns and change
- Use talk to organise, sequence and clarify thinking, ideas, feelings and events
- Extend their vocabulary, exploring the meanings and sounds of new words.

Background information/prior learning

Children have made ice lollies and been introduced to the words 'freeze' and 'melt'.

Introduction

Children will enjoy the snow outside, handling it and building people, houses, etc. They will look closely at snowflakes as they fall, 'catching' them on black paper.

Main activity

Children will collect snow in buckets and transfer it to the water tray. They will dig, build, mould and imprint and, as they play, will observe the snow melting. More snow will be introduced to the tray and the adult will offer children a jug of warm water to 'mix' with the snow. The adult will also introduce some large blocks of ice[5] (e.g. water frozen in margarine tubs) and encourage children to watch what happens to the snow when it is placed on an ice block.

Finishing off/follow-up
During the few days following the activity, small ice cubes containing objects such as pebbles, shells, buttons, beads and wedges of citrus fruit will be placed in the water tray. Children will collect the 'hidden' objects in a special container as the ice cubes melt. A balloon full of water (with a length of string inserted) will be frozen. The balloon 'skin' will then be removed and the 'ice balloon', on a string, made available to children.

Adult role
The adult will:

- Be prepared to respond immediately to the arrival of snow
- Prepare ice blocks and cubes in advance and store in readiness in the freezer
- Work alongside children, asking questions and introducing warm water/ice blocks at an appropriate time
- Model, and encourage use of, key vocabulary
- Observe children re: their observations, understanding of freezing/melting, use of key vocabulary.

Key questions and vocabulary
Vocabulary: Warm, cold, freeze, frozen, melt.
Questions: What does the snow feel like? How do your hands feel after holding the snow? What could you use to make a 'snow castle'? How long do you think a snowflake will stay on your hand? What do you think will happen to the snowball if we pour warm water onto it? What will happen to the warm water when it is mixed with the snow?

Resources

- Snow!
- Water tray, spades, buckets, plastic pots, shells, brushes, tubes, black paper
- Jugs of warm water (not too hot – safety is the paramount consideration. Tepid water will serve the purpose)
- Ice blocks
- Ice cubes (containing 'hidden' objects)

We need to feed the child's natural curiosity, the urge to explore, to try things out, to look more closely, to see what happens. We need to build on the child's disposition to explore and investigate, to satisfy the 'rage to know'.

(Fisher 1990)

---

[5] Take care that children do not 'burn' themselves on the ice.

CHAPTER 4

Establishing and developing positive links with home

Parents are children's first and most enduring educators. When parents and practitioners work together in early years settings, the results have a positive impact on the child's development and learning. Therefore, each setting should seek to develop an effective partnership with parents.

(QCA 2000)

The content of this chapter is organised as follows:

- First contact (p. 86)
- Planning and carrying out home visits (p. 87)
- The settling-in process (p. 89)
- Welcoming parents into the setting (p. 90)
- Planning home/setting 'link activities': introducing Oscar the clown (p. 92)
- Working with parents to support and extend children's learning (p. 96).

First contact

Prior to entering the setting, and during their early years, parents and the home environment will be central to a child's world and, in particular, to their emotional well-being. Many children will also have secured close bonds with professional carers, or carers within their family or circle of friends. Whatever the circumstances, for many children, starting nursery, preschool, playgroup, or beginning a new relationship with a childminder can be 'big milestones' in their lives. For both parents[1] and children, the prospect of entering this next stage, although exciting in many ways, is often tinged with apprehension.

The role of the practitioner is crucial in allaying anxieties and in building up trust between home and the setting. Experiences in the early days form the foundation for future attitudes and relationships.

A happy and open relationship with parents, based on confidence and trust, is crucial to the building of a successful relationship with their children.

(Whitebread 1996)

---

[1] From this point the word 'parents' will be used to refer to all main carers, whatever their relationship to the child.

It is important, then, that practitioners consider carefully how to ensure that children's and parents' initial contacts with staff and the setting are enjoyable experiences. Many settings organise induction or open days, or arrange visits to the setting, prior to the child's starting date. Parents and children will often be sent individual invitations and will be offered the opportunity to 'sample' activities while becoming familiar with staff and the physical surroundings. There may also be an explanation of the aims of the setting in the form of a talk by staff, perhaps illustrated by a slide show or displays.

Other practitioners visit children and parents in their own homes at times and dates mutually agreed beforehand. This system has the advantage of allowing both parties freedom from distractions and also provides a more intimate atmosphere in which parents may feel able to talk about concerns or personal circumstances that could affect the child. Young children will usually feel more relaxed and confident in familiar surroundings and visiting practitioners will find, in many cases, that the child sets the agenda, enthusiastically showing off toys and pets! However, practitioners should be aware that some parents may feel uneasy at the prospect of a home visit at this early stage in the relationship. This could be due to a number of factors, including negative experiences of education in their own childhood resulting in a lack of self-confidence or a mistrust of professionals. It is important to remember that the aim is to make the first contact between home and setting a positive experience, and the parent should always feel comfortable about the venue and nature of that first meeting – for this reason, any approach that is adopted by the practitioner, or team of practitioners, should be flexible.

If 'home visiting' is chosen as the preferred first contact, follow-up opportunities should also be planned for the child and parent to visit the setting before the official starting time; young children will feel more assured if they are able to visualise the provision and are familiar with some of the routines.

Planning and carrying out home visits

As any adult who works in an early years setting will appreciate, time is at a premium – there never seem to be enough hours in the day to fit all the jobs in! However, in the case of home visits, although there will be a limited amount of time available, it is important to allocate time slots long enough to enable relaxed conversations between adults, and interaction with the child, to take place. Many settings plan time during working hours for visits – some school nurseries close for two or three days at the beginning of each intake term to enable staff to make home visits, although this is not always possible. Whatever the arrangements, practitioners need to be well organised and prepared in order to ensure maximum benefit to all involved.

It is advisable for practitioners to visit in pairs, both from the safety aspect and also because this allows more flexibility during the visit. For example, a parent may want to talk about a serious issue concerning the child's health or safety – in the event of two adults being present, one could talk with the parent, recording any necessary information, while the other engages with the child. It is important to discuss and define roles prior to visiting and each adult needs to be clear about their responsibilities – it is too late, once out of the house, to discover that neither has established whether or not the child is 'toilet trained'!

Before embarking on visits, practitioners should always remember to inform an adult of their schedule – times of visits and addresses.

The following plan outlines some of the reasons for home visiting and offers suggestions for organisation, resources and the sharing of information. It is an example specific to one setting (arranging to carry out a number of visits over a period of a few days). Practitioners will need to tailor it to their own needs, may decide to adopt the framework for planning their visits, or may just choose to try out some of the ideas.

ORGANISING AND CARRYING OUT HOME VISITS

Dates: 5–8 September.

Duration of each visit: 30 minutes.

Aims of each visit

- To establish positive links between home and the setting
- To begin to develop a relationship between the child and staff
- To familiarise the parent with the aims of the setting – policies, routines, etc.
- To enable staff to become aware of child's home circumstances and relevant prior experiences
- To informally assess child's stage of development and readiness for the setting

Resources needed

- List of names, telephone numbers and addresses; timetable of visits
- Street map of local area
- Home visit record forms/questionnaires[2]
- Photograph album – a collection of annotated photographs showing children at play in the setting
- Soft toy character – 'Oscar' the clown (see Figure 4.2, p. 92)
- Small present for the child (e.g. drawing book and crayons)
- Booklet containing information about the setting
- 'About Me' leaflet[2]

Organisation and adult role

Arranging visits:

- Contact families to confirm that a visit is required and to arrange a suitable time.
- Ensure that all information in booklets is correct and up to date.
- Check that there are sufficient forms, booklets, etc. for every visit.
- Gather all resources together, compiling individual packs of leaflets, forms, booklets, etc. in labelled bags.

Carrying out the visits:

- Introduce staff by name to the parent and child.

---

[2]   See chapter 6 for details of contents and purpose of forms, questionnaires and leaflets.

- Talk with, and listen to, the child, putting her/him at ease (use props ' photograph album, the drawing equipment and 'Oscar' the clown to conversation).
- Observe, in particular, the child's social, physical and language skills.
- Explain to the parent, for example, how the setting/staffing is organised, strategies for settling children into the setting, routines, systems of assessment, how information is communicated between staff and parents, and rotas for parent help in the setting. Show the parent the photograph album and talk about activities.
- Ask the parent if there are any questions she/he would like to ask, information that needs to be shared (if this has not already been recorded on a form or questionnaire) or any issues/concerns that ought to be discussed.
- Inform the parent of any equipment the child will need, such as a spare set of clothes, inside shoes.
- Ask standard questions (if these have not already been answered during the course of conversation) and complete records.
- Remind the parent that he/she is welcome to visit the setting, with the child, prior to the official starting date.

Following up visits:

- Plan starting dates for children, staggered if necessary.
- Inform parents of the official starting date for their children.
- Prepare individual equipment such as name cards, milk tags, coat peg labels.
- Begin each child's profile (see chapter 6, p. 138) by making a 'home visit' entry.

The settling-in process

Children's responses to starting their new setting will vary enormously. Some will enter on the first day full of enthusiasm and confidence and eager to explore. Others will be much more reticent, preferring to observe from a 'safe' distance. Many may cope with a full session or day while some will benefit from shorter sessions in the beginning. Every child is different and practitioners must take their lead from the individual when devising programmes for 'settling in'.

Settings also vary as to what is an appropriate or practical approach. In a situation where all 'foundation-stage' children are together in a unit, transition into 'reception' should not cause any problems. But if children are arriving from other settings, reception-class staff will find that children usually settle more easily if links are made with settings attended prior to starting school. The transition period should be carefully planned to allow children opportunities to experience activities in the class (e.g. an invitation to a story session, or to lunch) and, where possible, should include visits by reception staff to children in their own setting or home (see home visits, p. 87). Similar transition arrangements should also be planned for children transferring from one setting to another at an earlier point during the foundation stage.

As a general rule, for three-year-olds starting in a new setting, parents should be encouraged to stay with their child for at least the first session, and for parts of, or complete, subsequent sessions until the child is settled. It may be that the child is happy to venture away from the parent immediately, in which case the parent may decide to keep their distance, within the setting, on the first day. After observing the child's behaviour the parent may feel confident in leaving the child for a short period the next day. Invariably the child will soon be entering the setting confidently and be happy to wave 'goodbye' to the parent as soon as the routines have been completed. However, it does sometimes happen that a seemingly very confident child becomes 'clingy' after a few days in the setting, as if the novelty of the experience has worn rather thin. In such a case the practitioner and parent will need to review the situation and may decide that the child needs more support than originally anticipated.

Occasionally, a child will be happy to play with other children and explore the setting with a parent present but, even after a period of time, will be extremely reluctant for the parent to leave. It may be that the child is anxious about the possibility of the parent not returning. The child should not feel under pressure to 'make the break' before feeling ready and, in order to build up the child's confidence, the separation process will need to progress in small steps. The 'break' can also prove to be emotionally difficult for the parent, who may need support and understanding from the practitioner. Perhaps, on the first day of separation, the parent could sit in another room in the same building for ten minutes – some settings are fortunate enough to have permanent access to a parents' room. The length of time could be built up gradually over a period of a few days until both parent and child feel comfortable about the parent leaving the building for part of the session. As the child realises that the parent always comes back, he or she will become less anxious about the separation, eventually feeling happy to attend the whole session without the parent being present.

Many settings operate a system of 'key workers' – each child will have a member of staff 'assigned' to them and that adult will be responsible for greeting the child at the beginning of each session, spending time working with, and observing, the child during the session and liaising with parents. This can help the child to feel secure in the setting and often accelerates the process of settling in. Key workers may also be responsible for recording and reporting the achievements and progress of the children in their group.

The crucial word in the process is 'trust'. When a child is let down by an adult, the bond of trust will be damaged and the child will feel insecure. Adults must be consistent, reliable and truthful – a child should always be told when a parent is about to leave the setting and when he or she will return. Slipping out of the door while the child is temporarily preoccupied, or distorting the truth about where they are going, are not actions conducive to building up a relationship of trust with a child. Practitioners should make time to talk with the parent about the child's progress, listening and responding to any concerns – the trust that develops between practitioner and parent during these early days is sure to impact positively on the development of the child.

Welcoming parents into the setting

It is the policy of most settings to encourage parents to spend time in the setting throughout their child's time there, and some parents are able and happy to come in on a regular basis.

There is often an abundance of strengths and enthusiasms to be 'tapped' amongst the parents and carers – some may be able to play musical instruments, others will have a particular interest in woodwork, sewing or gardening. Whatever skills they have to offer, the practitioner should encourage them to share them with the children in the setting. There are numerous other activities, many of them on-going, with which parents can become involved on a day-to-day basis, such as reading stories with the children, making models, building dens, baking, teaching routines in the painting area, and joining in imaginative and role play in the home corner.

Beginning-of-session routines, such as self-registration systems and the 'question table', provide a focus for children and parents on entry to the setting, as well-offering sound learning opportunities for the child. Self-registration usually involves the child, supported by the parent, in taking a label or tag (displaying a personal motif or photograph of self and/or name) and placing it in a designated place in order to register the child's presence in the setting. The labels may be hanging on coat pegs when the children arrive, or may be arranged on a table, requiring children to select their own cards. The label may then, for example, be hung over a milk bottle or a named photograph attached with self-adhesive hook-and-loop fastening tape to a train or house displayed on the wall. A glance at the labels will inform the practitioner of which children are present. Details of the 'question table' are included in chapter 5, pp. 112–113.

Practitioners may also decide to organise social events and these are often run alongside planned activities involving the children, such as a Christmas concert or 'sing-along' accompanied by coffee and mince pies. Such occasions offer parents opportunities to meet other parents and to chat informally with staff. It is advisable to give plenty of notice when planning events of this nature to allow parents with other commitments to make the necessary arrangements in order to attend. In many settings parents organise fundraising or social events themselves, and this kind of involvement can be beneficial in helping to bind the partnership between practitioner and parent, as well as in providing very worthwhile experiences for all.

Parents are often invited to share experiences with their children and Figure 4.1 illustrates an example of such an occasion. Parents were invited to the nursery to meet 'Eeyore', a visiting donkey. Eeyore was accompanied by staff from the local donkey centre who talked to children and parents about caring for donkeys and the work of the Elisabeth Svendsen Trust for Children and Donkeys. The children were enthralled and eager to talk about their experiences. Because of the parents' involvement, they were able to discuss the visit with their children in detail, and with enthusiasm. The nursery decided to 'adopt' a donkey (on a sponsorship basis) from the centre and parents were very supportive. Parents, children and staff now had a shared commitment to the

Figure 4.1 Eeyore's visit to nursery

charity, which not only benefited the Trust, but also served to strengthen links between home and setting.

The setting itself should feel welcoming to the parent. Provision (a safe distance from the children's play area) of tea- and coffee-making facilities and an area where parents can sit comfortably and talk will be an attraction. Not all parents want to spend time working with children in the setting and some find it difficult because of caring for younger siblings, but they may be happy to offer their support by making or cataloguing resources – a 'working party' could be set up, for example, to make up story boxes or catalogue posters. Although the practitioner would be involved in the content of the work, parents could organise the rota and decide responsibilities for tasks. This can be a very successful way of involving parents in the curriculum and can also have positive social repercussions for many. The provision of a box of toys suitable for younger children and babies is also a good idea – parents will often be happy to contribute to this collection. Parents can be involved in the organisation of a book- and toy-lending library within the setting, sharing responsibility for the smooth running of the system, and for the maintenance of the resources, with the practitioner.

A 'parents' notice board' is an effective way of communicating information to parents, such as forthcoming events in the setting, new staff appointed to work in the setting and holiday dates. Useful leaflets about local facilities such as clinics, support groups and toy libraries can also be displayed and the board can be used by parents to inform each other about happenings in the community, such as school fairs, jumble sales and aerobics classes. The provision of such a board will help to give parents a feeling of inclusion in the setting, will encourage social interaction between parents and will also convey the message that the setting does not work in isolation – that it is an integral part of the community.

Practitioners may also decide to take information (such as a summary of aims, session times, dates of open days and social events) about the setting into the wider community, displaying posters or leaflets in libraries, doctors' surgeries and clinics. This will serve to raise awareness of the setting in the community and encourage prospective parents to visit.

Planning home/setting 'link activities': introducing Oscar the clown

Working parents, and parents with other demanding commitments, are not always able to enjoy the frequent contact with the setting that they would like, but it is possible to plan activities involving parents and children that take place in the home.

The visit of a soft-toy character to the setting is a reliable way of engaging children and stimulating their imagination. This approach has already been suggested in the focus activity 'Lion's visit' (see chapter 3, p. 64), during which a friendly lion spends time in the setting and challenges children to build him a den. The example used in this chapter is of 'Oscar' (Figure 4.2), a brightly coloured, well-travelled clown who has, to date,

Figure 4.2 Oscar with his suitcase

visited approximately 150 homes in Leeds and been well cared for in all!

The aim of the 'Oscar' project is to develop children's learning in the areas of personal, social and emotional development and communication, language and literacy, and also to help develop positive links between home and the setting. If introduced at a time when new children are joining the setting, Oscar can also help to ease the settling-in process for children. For example, he could 'befriend' children who are feeling a little unsure; children could take responsibility for looking after Oscar while he is 'new' in the setting; they could explain a new activity to him, show him around the setting or merely invite him to watch as they play. The project is an idea that can easily be used in any setting, with little or no adaptation, and it is popular with both children and parents.

The plan of Oscar's visit is presented in the same format as the focus activities cited in previous chapters.

ACTIVITY:
OSCAR THE CLOWN VISITS CHILDREN IN THEIR OWN HOMES

Focus areas of learning

- Personal, social and emotional development
- Communication, language and literacy

Learning objectives

- To develop a sense of responsibility
- To be aware of the needs of others
- To take turns
- To gain confidence in sharing experiences and expressing feelings in a group situation
- To listen and respond to other children's accounts of their experiences
- To understand that writing carries meaning
- To attempt writing to convey meaning
- To reinforce and develop links with home
- For parents and children to share in an experience initiated in the setting

Working towards QCA early learning goals
By the end of the foundation stage, most children will:

- Continue to be interested, excited and motivated to learn
- Be confident to try new activities, initiate ideas and speak in a familiar group
- Have a developing awareness of their own needs, views and feelings and be sensitive to the needs, views and feelings of others
- Work as part of a group or class, taking turns and sharing fairly, understanding that there need to be agreed codes of behaviour for groups of people, including adults and children, to work together harmoniously
- Dress and undress independently and manage their own personal hygiene.

(Personal, social and emotional development)

By the end of the foundation stage, most children will be able to:

- Use talk to organise, sequence and clarify thinking, ideas, feelings and events
- Sustain attentive listening, responding to what they have heard by relevant comments, questions or actions
- Know that print carries meaning and, in English, is read from left to right and top to bottom
- Attempt writing for various purposes, using features of different forms such as lists, stories and instructions.

(Communication, language and literacy)

Background information/prior learning

Children may have been introduced to Oscar during a home visit (see the 'home visit plan', p. 88). Children and staff will have talked about personal hygiene, and in particular the need for washing, brushing teeth and combing hair.

Introduction

The adult will gather together a group of children on the first day of the 'Oscar' project. Oscar will be introduced to the children and they will be shown his suitcase and its contents (see 'resources'). The leading adult will explain that Oscar has come to spend time in the setting and needs somewhere to sleep at night. Some time for discussion and suggestions will be allowed. The adult will then tell the children that Oscar would like to stay for a night at each of their homes and will read an entry in his diary describing his visit to the home of a member of staff. They will discuss the care of Oscar with a focus on personal hygiene and safety.

Main activity

Every day Oscar will go home with a different child. The child will be encouraged to care for Oscar, to share toys/experiences with him and to talk about photographs in his album. Parents will receive a letter of explanation, asked to participate and, with the child, to make an entry in Oscar's diary.

Finishing off/follow-up

In the weekly planning, time will be allocated for daily discussion of Oscar's visits to children's homes. Following each of Oscar's 'home visits', the child concerned will show the group the diary and talk about his/her experiences with the clown. Other children will be encouraged to ask the child questions about Oscar's visit. Photographs, letters to Oscar, diary entries and so on will be displayed in the setting (on boards or made into books).

Adult role

The adult will:

- Provide resources – check contents of the suitcase after every visit
- Stimulate interest in the activity during the introduction
- Write a letter explaining the activity. Give a copy of the letter, and talk about the activity, to parents when it is their child's turn to take Oscar
- Support and encourage children as they talk about Oscar's visit to their houses
- Read entries in Oscar's diary
- Ensure that all children are given the opportunity to take Oscar home.

Key questions

Why do you think Oscar has come to the nursery? What do you think he would like to play with? Where will he sleep tonight? Do you think he will be lonely in the setting by himself? Do you think Oscar would like to sleep at your house? How would you look after him? Which of your toys would you show him? What did you and Oscar do yesterday evening? Which other members of your family did Oscar meet? Did he remember to brush his teeth before he went to bed? Did you show him how to comb his hair? What did you and Oscar eat for your tea? Shall we read your entry in Oscar's diary? Would you like to read what you have written? Which part of Oscar's visit did you enjoy the most?

Resources

- Oscar (soft-toy clown)
- Oscar's suitcase containing: his diary, photograph album (see Figure 4.3), favourite toy, toothbrush, comb, a pencil and a letter from Oscar[3] addressed to the child
- Letter to parents – a brief explanation of the aims of the project and the required involvement from the parent

Figure 4.3 One of the pictures from Oscar's photograph album

Monday

Today Oscar came home with Natalia and she was very excited. He sat at the table at lunch time and ate cheese sandwiches with her. After lunch we all went to the post office and Natalia carried Oscar all the way. Oscar helped Natalia to post some letters and then we all came home. Oscar and Natalia played with toys for the rest of the afternoon. We went to Auntie Di's for tea – pasta, Natalia's favourite. At bed time, Natalia helped Oscar to clean his teeth and wash his face. Then they both brushed their hair and went to bed.

Figure 4.4 Natalia's entry in Oscar's diary: Mum and Natalia's writing – Natalia's writing reads 'Oscar came to play at my house'

Figure 4.5 Natalia's drawing – 'Me and Oscar and Mummy'

---

[3] Content will include, for example, a 'thank you' for inviting him to stay, information about his favourite food, activities and toys, a list of items packed in his suitcase and a reminder to take care of him and to return him (with all belongings!) the following day.

Children will often take Oscar with them to the supermarket, café, park, Grandma's house, the fair – some have even taken him on holiday for the weekend (see Figure 4.6) and come back with very exciting tales to tell about his adventures!

Figure 4.6 Oscar enjoys a family holiday with Laura and George

Working with parents to support and extend children's learning

In acknowledging parents as the child's 'first and most enduring educators' (QCA 2000), practitioners must recognise that their own role is inextricably linked to that of parents. The learning process does not take place exclusively in the setting, nor does it only happen at home – experiences in all aspects of children's lives combine to broaden and deepen their learning. It is the role of the practitioner and parent to support the child in that process.

Parent and practitioners have much to learn from each other and an efficient system of communication should be in operation to facilitate the sharing of information. This will involve both parties in making time to talk and listen. Experience and training will equip the practitioner with the professional expertise needed to plan an appropriate and broad curriculum within the setting. But their expertise can have a wider impact when their approach includes involvement of parents in the planned curriculum. This section of the chapter focuses on building an effective partnership between parents and practitioners as educators.

It is worth mentioning at this point the many commercially produced resources on the market that claim to be aids to 'home learning', some of which can be useful if carefully selected. Some, however, are at best 'gimmicks' and, at worst, inappropriate for the child's stage of development and likely to lead to bad practice or confusion. Parents eager to give their child the best educational start in life are vulnerable to marketing ploys and are frequently persuaded to spend large amounts of money on so-called educational toys, videos and 'workbooks' of dubious quality. The reality is that, very often, equally or more valuable learning experiences can take place at little or no expense in the home or local environment. Practitioners have an important role to play here in sharing their expertise and knowledge of how young children learn, in helping parents to interpret their children's play in terms of learning, and in offering suggestions of how learning can be supported at home. It may be appropriate to point out that children's learning should be contextual and purposeful, and to emphasise the value of conversation between adult and child.

Many parents will be keen to learn more about the early years curriculum and the activities planned for their children. An effective way of sharing ideas and curricular aims in a relaxed atmosphere is to hold an open day or evening and to invite parents to have 'hands-on experience' of activities (some settings may organise a similar event prior to children starting the setting). Practitioners would be available to talk about children's play and learning, and to answer questions. A brief explanation of learning objectives, and photographs of children engaging in a range of activities, displayed in each area of provision can also provide some helpful information.

> Parents are particularly predisposed to understand play and its learning potential if invited to curriculum or topic sessions in school and allowed to experience for themselves some of the materials and resources children use.

> (Moyles 1989)

Some practitioners produce guidance leaflets for parents.[4] These can help to explain the learning that takes place in the setting, and can also be a very welcome support to those helping in the setting. However, practitioners should guard against overwhelming the parent with too much 'paperwork' – information should be useful, concise, easy to read and attractively presented. The content may be of a general nature (e.g. explanation of routines, areas limited to four children at a time, encouraging independence) but can also be specific to an area of provision, including information such as suggested activities, and ways in which the adult can support children's learning across the curriculum in, for example, the sand area. Reference to long-term plans may help practitioners in writing 'area-of-provision' leaflets.

Leaflets may also be produced that focus on the six areas of learning. These will offer information on how learning in a particular curricular area can be developed in different areas of provision (see Figure 4.7).

Many practitioners plan focus activities and learning experiences within the setting around a particular interest or theme (e.g. ourselves, festivals) and the duration of such 'units' will vary. Other settings may choose to look at a particular area of learning (e.g. creative development) and focus on how children's learning can be developed in that area over a period of, for example, three weeks. Whatever the starting point for medium-term planning, if practitioners inform parents of the content, and suggest home activities that will support the planned learning, the curriculum can be significantly enriched for the child. Once aware of the practitioner's plans, many parents will have exciting ideas of their own for developing their children's learning and should be encouraged to share these. Information can be displayed on a board in the setting or can be communicated through a letter from the staff, as illustrated in Figure 4.8. Practitioners may decide to include other information on the letter, such as notification of a planned coffee morning, or they may choose to produce separate 'news' letters.

Often children will go home at the end of the session proudly clutching a pile of paintings, drawings and models. This is to be encouraged and such works of art are usually received with enthusiasm by parents. However, not all learning has a tangible 'end product' and it is important that the value of the learning process, and the conceptual achievements, are also understood by parents.

Although practitioners aim to share information verbally about children's experiences on a daily basis, it can be helpful (particularly to parents who are unable to have daily contact with the setting) sometimes to send home at the end of the day a brief written explanation of an activity enjoyed by a child. This will be especially useful in the absence

---

[4] These leaflets can also be useful to other adults working in the setting (e.g. students, new staff).

MATHEMATICAL DEVELOPMENT IN THE NURSERY

You can support children's mathematical development in all areas of the setting. Listed below are some suggested activities:

- *Construction area:* looking at and comparing shapes of bricks; matching shapes to templates; sorting components (by colour, shape or size); counting the amount of component parts used to make a model.
- *Painting area:* printing flat shapes; creating or recreating patterns and sequences looking at colour, size and shape.
- *Malleable materials:* making solid shapes; comparing length (who has made the longest snake?); sharing the dough (three children: three amounts of dough).
- *Home corner:* matching 1:1 e.g. laying the table – spoon, cup, saucer for each child; shopping – dealing with money; counting/matching numbered clothes on a washing line; knock four times on the door before entering; counting candles on a birthday cake.
- *Office:* reading and dialling telephone numbers; writing numbers (e.g. house numbers on envelopes); matching numbered stamps to numbered postboxes.
- *Water area:* comparing containers (shape and size); filling and emptying containers; counting the number of jugs of water needed to fill a bowl.
- *Music area:* using instruments to explore rhythm – counting beats; clapping names (e.g. Sam – an – tha, 1 – 2 – 3); singing number songs e.g. 'Five Little Speckled Frogs'.
- *Sand area:* looking at solid shapes – using cuboids as moulds (wet sand); filling and emptying containers with sand; feeling sand paper numbers on the wall; ordering size-graded containers; weighing bags of sand.
- *Workshop area:* comparing/measuring lengths of wood; solving problems (e.g. how long does the piece of string need to be to go around the box?).
- *Book area:* looking at fiction and non-fiction books which involve e.g. counting, size/shape/height/length comparison; listening to number rhyme audio tapes.

Talking with the children as they play helps to develop their mathematical understanding as well as their language. They should be encouraged to use the following vocabulary and will learn the meaning of words through hearing you use them:

Number: 1, 2, 3, 4, 5, 6, 7, 8, 9, 10 (higher number names if children are ready).
Shape: circle, square, triangle, rectangle, cylinder, sphere, cuboid, cone.
Size: big, bigger, small, smaller.
Length/height: long, longer, short, shorter, tall, taller.
Weight: heavy, heavier, light, lighter.
Capacity: full, fuller, empty, emptier.
Pattern: same, different, next to.

There are also a number of computer programmes available that support children's mathematical learning. A member of staff will be happy to talk about these with you.

Figure 4.7 Mathematical development in the nursery – guidance leaflet

---

of an 'end product' to the activity. The production of a photocopiable pro forma (to which individual observations can be added) for use during focus activities reduces the length of time taken to record the information (see Figure 4.9). Where practitioners have access to a photocopier in the setting, written observations of spontaneous activities (intended for inclusion in profiles) could occasionally be photocopied and a copy sent to the parent with a standard explanation note attached. Such information may prove to be a useful prompt for children who, when asked about the day's activities, invariably respond with the easiest answer: 'Nothing', or perhaps, 'I don't know'! Although persistent questioning is unlikely to be the right course of action in such a situation, having some information about a particular activity will enable the parent to more effectively engage in conversation with

First Steps Nursery

'GROWTH AND LIVING THINGS'

Dear Parents and Carers,

Now that spring is with us, we will be looking particularly at 'growth and living things' with the children. We have planned some exciting activities including:

- Observing the life-cycle of a butterfly and a frog (caterpillars and frogspawn are due to arrive next week – look out for the 'Living Things' display!).
- A visit to a local farm (parents and carers will be invited to join us – details to follow).
- A search for 'mini-beasts' in the outside play area.
- Growing a range of vegetables and flowers, observing and measuring their growth.
- A visit from a health visitor, talking about keeping healthy.

There are many ways in which you can help to develop your child's learning about 'growth and living things' at home. Here are a few suggestions from us – please let us know about your good ideas so that we can share them with other parents!

- A visit to the park looking at, and talking about, leaves, buds, flowers, insects.
- Making a scrapbook of things found in the park.
- A visit to the local garden centre to look at plants, seedlings, trees, shrubs.
- Digging and planting – there are many plants that will happily grow in pots on a window sill if access to a garden or 'allotment' is difficult. (Cut-off carrot tops in a saucer of water quickly grow shoots and require little attention!)
- Talking about pets – how they have changed as they have grown, and the care they need.
- Talking about their own growth and the food/care they need to be healthy.
- Looking at photographs of themselves (from babyhood to present day).

Thank you for your cooperation – have fun investigating with your child!

The nursery staff.

Figure 4.8 Letter to parents: 'Growth and living things'

Today we have read a story called 'Handa's Surprise' in which Handa decides to take a basket full of exotic fruits to her friend as a present.

We have been tasting some of these fruits in nursery.

_____Daniel_____

liked _mango and pineapple_____

disliked _passion fruit and tangerine_

Figure 4.9 Explanation of 'tasting exotic fruits' activity

the child about that activity, asking informed and focused questions. It will also help to raise the status of activities with no 'end product' as valuable learning experiences.

The provision of information such as play-dough recipes, instructions on how to make a sock puppet and lists of useful resources to include in a 'junk modelling box' at home will be appreciated by many parents. Children may also be asked to bring resources from home to support learning in the setting, such as 'junk' materials (e.g. cereal boxes, cardboard tubes, yoghurt pots) for model-making in the workshop, items for an 'interest' table (e.g. natural forms, objects of a particular colour), or photographs of themselves as babies for a display on 'growing up'.

Children's achievements are often summarised more formally at intervals during, and/or at the end of, their time in the setting in the form of written 'records of achievement' for parents. These are looked at in more detail in chapter 6, but it is worth mentioning here the importance of giving parents opportunities to respond to, and discuss, the information included in such reports. Time should be planned for practitioners to talk, undisturbed (as far as possible!), with parents about their child's progress.

> Conversations with parents can benefit all parties concerned. It benefits teachers because of their increased knowledge of the child, it benefits parents by making them genuine partners in their child's learning and it benefits children, who see home and school as mutually interested in their education.
>
> (Fisher 1996)

The two-way flow of information between practitioner and parent about the child is a vital aspect of the partnership. Children's achievements at home and in the setting should be celebrated, as well as concerns voiced, and parents should feel comfortable in approaching staff. If the content of the discussion is of a sensitive nature, it will need to be conducted in privacy and confidentiality respected. Children's 'profiles' are another way in which practitioner and parent can combine information to give a more complete picture of the child's learning achievements. The purposes of profiles, and methods of compiling them, are looked at in chapter 6.

It should be the aim of all key adults in a child's life to build an effective network system through which they can communicate information to support the child in making progress in all areas of learning. Sharing the knowledge that each of those adults has about the child is essential in addressing the needs of the 'whole child'.

> Nursery education should throughout be an affair of cooperation between the nursery and home and it will only succeed to the full if it carries the parents into partnership.
>
> (Department of Education and Science 1967, para. 32)

CHAPTER 5

Planning display as part of the curriculum

Displays are focal points for learning.

(Lancaster 1987)

The content of this chapter is organised as follows:

- Planning a display (p. 101)
- Display can be interactive (p. 103)
- Display can celebrate (p. 118)
- Display can be informative (p. 123)
- Constructing displays: some practical hints (p. 124).

The aim of this chapter is to define the purpose of display and to offer guidance in providing high-quality display that will be an integral part of the learning environment and make a positive contribution to the children's development in all areas.

Why construct a display?

There are a number of reasons why a practitioner may decide to construct a display in the setting, including:

- To celebrate children's achievements
- To stimulate children's interest and/or imagination
- To engage children in an activity
- To extend children's knowledge in a particular area
- To provide information for adults.

Planning a display

It is not necessary, in most cases, to write a full plan for a display although this can be helpful in some circumstances and these are discussed later in the chapter. It is, however, essential for all adults in the setting to be aware of the aims of the display and its proposed uses. It is a good idea to discuss display plans as a team, and asking questions in order to clarify purpose can be a useful exercise. For example:

- What is the learning focus of the display?
- Who will benefit from the display?
- What will they learn?

Having determined the reasons for constructing the display, the practitioner can then decide on the most appropriate methods of organisation and presentation. There will be a multitude of alternatives and decisions will, again, be influenced to a large extent by practicalities and physical features of the setting. Practitioners may not have access to permanent wallboards, shelving or suitable surfaces and will need to think about how to provide portable displays, which can be stored away between sessions. Folding screens can be very useful pieces of equipment in such circumstances, as can wheeled storage units (with a surface at child level), portable frameworks (from which to hang children's work, objects of interest, etc.), free-standing open shelving and 'sandwich'-style boards.

Throughout this chapter, examples of displays will be categorised as:

- *Wall:* this will refer to all displays fixed to a vertical surface (e.g. wall-mounted boards, free-standing boards, screens)
- *Table top:* including all horizontal surfaces (e.g. tops of cupboards, large trays or boards)
- *Shelf:* open shelving, fixed or free standing
- *Suspended:* pieces of work or objects displayed by hanging them from a framework or permanent fixture in the setting.

Whatever the type of display, it should be easily accessible to the child visually and (if appropriate) physically. This means making sure that displays are at a comfortable height for children and also that there is ample space around each for children to look at, or work with, displayed items. When the intended audience consists solely of adults, wall displays should be at adult eye level.

The length of time a display stays in the setting is dependent on its purpose. Some displays will be constructed spontaneously, perhaps in response to children's immediate interests, and these may only be applicable for a brief period of time. Others are set up to complement work planned around a theme. Such displays may need to remain in the setting long enough for children to observe changes (e.g. tadpoles into frogs, seeds into plants during a 'growth and living things' topic) or may be altered by the practitioner at intervals during the 'topic' (e.g. if the planned learning is focused on 'books', the 'Looking at Books' display could be changed weekly to cover fiction, poetry, non-fiction or to celebrate the work of different authors). If a display is intended to engage children in an activity, ample time should be allowed for them to return to the activity, perhaps a number of times, to review or modify work and for reinforcement of concepts.

It may be that the display informs children about, for example, the different resources permanently on offer in an area of provision, in which case there would be justification for an extended period of display, as the relevance of that information is 'on-going'. The practitioner should, however, be aware that display that becomes a 'permanent fixture' in the setting will probably cease to attract children's attention, or hold their interest, and its effectiveness may be significantly reduced after a certain period of time. (This may not be the case if adult time is regularly given to using long-term displays with children.) In any event, displays that are faded, 'tatty' or no longer complete are not going to inspire children to learn and should be dismantled.

In order to look in more depth at the different purposes and aspects of display, the next part of the chapter is divided into three sections and explores ways in which display can be interactive, can celebrate work and can be informative. In practice many displays will, and should, include elements from two or all of these categories, but examples have been selected according to their dominant purpose.

Display can be interactive

Interactive display can engage children physically and intellectually. It can actively involve children in first-hand learning experiences and challenge them, through questions and provision of appropriate and stimulating resources, to:

- Solve problems
- Design and build or make for a specific purpose (functional or fantasy)
- Find out (specific information/open ended)
- Follow instructions
- Have, and share, opinions
- Develop imaginative ideas
- Record information, observations, findings and imaginative ideas.

The display may target a key area of learning or combine learning in two or three areas through a common theme. There may be a very specific intended outcome, or learning may be more open ended, the emphasis being on experimentation, exploration and investigation through the senses. Interactive display can also encourage collaborative and cooperative work. Whatever the intended learning, for valuable experiences to be assured, practitioners must give high priority to planning the display.

Interactive display is one type of display where a more structured approach to planning will probably benefit both the practitioner and the children. Display of this nature should be regarded rather like a focus activity in that learning goals should be clearly defined and resources carefully selected. The adult role is also an important issue to be discussed by the team. During the period of time that the display is available, children will probably have free access to it and adults will need to intervene and support as appropriate. For this reason, all adults involved in the setting need to be aware of how to effectively support children working at the display from the time of its introduction. The nature of the support will vary from display to display, and child to child. The practitioner may need to focus on supporting the child in using the display independently, or may need to offer more direct learning support. Intervention will often be spontaneous, but there will probably be occasions when practitioners will want to plan time slots in the weekly planning for adult input, particularly to introduce the display (see 'leaf investigation', p. 109) and to develop learning potential.

The main reason for producing a full, written plan for an interactive display is to inform, and remind, adults of its focus and objectives as and when they consider it appropriate to offer their support to children using the display. Plans will need to be easily accessible to adults and preferably displayed alongside the interactive display. They can also be a useful practical prompt for practitioners when repeating a display and gathering resources.

The following two plans are offered as examples. The reader will note that, although both displays fall into the category of 'interactive display', each sets different expectations in terms of children's use of resources. The 'shape and colour decision tree' is quite specific in its guidance, offering a series of instructions that will focus children's learning on some specific objectives. In the second example, the 'exploring sound' display, activities are of a more investigative nature and learning intentions more open ended.

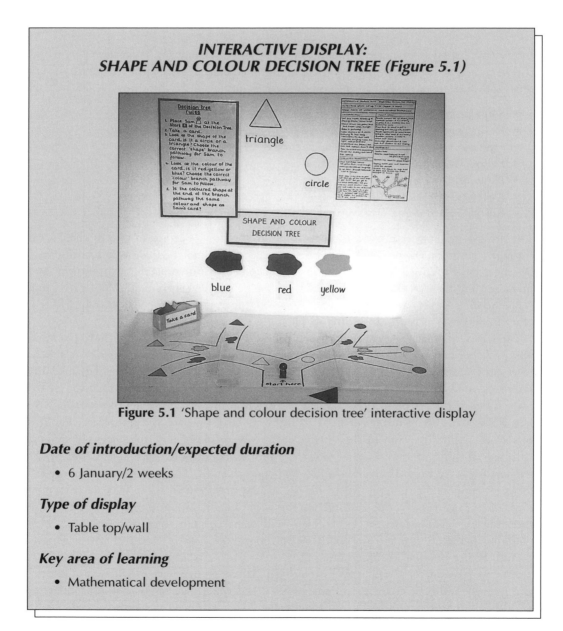

Figure 5.1 'Shape and colour decision tree' interactive display

Date of introduction/expected duration

- 6 January/2 weeks

Type of display

- Table top/wall

Key area of learning

- Mathematical development

Learning objectives

- To match/recognise/name key colours and shapes
- To make decisions according to given criteria
- To develop logical thinking and to follow pathways

Working towards QCA early learning goals in mathematical development

By the end of the foundation stage, most children will be able to:

- Use language such as 'circle' or 'bigger' to describe the shape and size of solids and flat shapes
- Use everyday words to describe position
- Use developing mathematical ideas and methods to solve practical problems.

Resources

- Horizontal surface and wall space or vertical board
- Decision cards (coloured shapes – red, yellow, blue /circle, triangle) in a box
- Colour and shape labels
- 'Sam' doll
- Decision tree drawn on large sheet of card[1]
- Decision tree instructions for use with/by children
- Copy of display plan (for adult)

Activities

Children will:

- Select a card and look at its shape
- Decide which shape 'branch' to take – circle or triangle
- Follow the branch (with the card or 'Sam' doll) until it divides
- Look at the colour of the card
- Decide which colour 'branch' to take – blue, red or yellow
- Follow the branch to its limit
- Compare the coloured shape at the end of the branch with the one on the card selected – is it the same?

Adult role

The adult will:

- Set up the display and check resources daily
- Introduce the display to children, explaining objectives
- Plan time for adult input (observing, and working with, children)
- Spontaneously support children as appropriate, modelling use of key vocabulary and asking questions.

---

[1] It is helpful to include a diagram of the layout of the decision tree at this point (see Figure 5.2).

Key vocabulary and questions

Vocabulary: Colour and shape names (e.g. 'red', 'blue', 'yellow', 'circle', 'triangle'); positional/directional language (e.g. 'up', 'down', 'forwards', 'backwards', 'next to', 'between').

Questions: What colour is the circle? What shape is your card? Can you tell me two things about your card? (colour/shape) Have you got the same shape as your friend? Look at the shape of your card – which branch should you choose? Does your card match the coloured shape at the end of your chosen 'route'? Did you go the right way? Did you get to the right place? Where do you think you made a mistake? Do you think you would get to the same place with a different card? Where do you think this card would lead you? Can you explain the 'decision tree' rules to your friend?

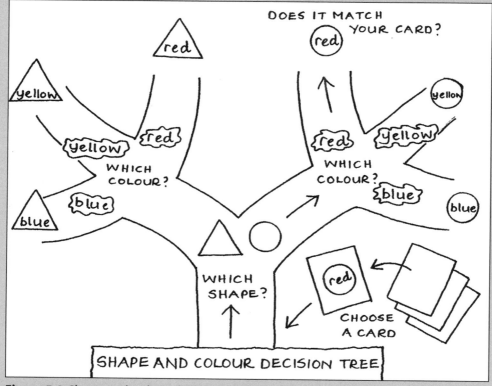

Figure 5.2 Shape and colour decision tree

INTERACTIVE DISPLAY: EXPLORING SOUND

Date of introduction/expected duration

- 10 June/3 weeks

Type of display

- Table top/suspended

Key areas of learning

- Creative development
- Knowledge and understanding of the world

Learning objectives

- To listen to, and discriminate between, a variety of sounds
- To experiment with materials to produce different sounds
- To relate sounds to animals, and to use musical instruments to express characteristics such as size, nature and movement

Working towards QCA early learning goals in key areas
By the end of the foundation stage, most children will be able to:

- Recognise and explore how sounds can be changed, sing simple songs from memory, recognise repeated sounds and sound patterns and match movements to music
- Express and communicate their ideas, thoughts and feelings by using a widening range of materials, suitable tools, imaginative and role play, movement, designing and making, and a variety of songs and musical instruments

(Creative development)

- Investigate objects and materials by using all of their senses as appropriate.

(Knowledge and understanding of the world)

Resources

- A range of musical instruments including commercially produced instruments, instruments made by adults and children in the setting, instruments from other cultures
- Copper piping (cut to different lengths) suspended (to hang at different levels) from a large wire lampshade frame hung from the ceiling. Additional lengths of metal and plastic piping, wooden sticks and fabric-covered sticks provided for use by children to 'play' the hanging pipes
- A range of materials with which children can make their own instruments (e.g. cardboard boxes, rubber bands, yoghurt pots, margarine pots, cardboard tubes, pieces of fabric, sand, dried peas)

- A box of 'animal cards' – photographs of animals to be used as prompts for children when relating sounds to animals (e.g. lion, mouse, elephant, sparrow)
- Fiction/non-fiction books about musical instruments
- A board (to be used as a screen)

Activities
Children will:

- Handle commercially produced, and other, instruments
- Listen to, and compare sounds made by, different instruments
- Talk about their observations using key vocabulary and descriptive language
- With an adult or friend, play sound-matching games (play the instrument behind a screen and ask your friend to guess what is making the sound)
- Experiment with sound using one instrument – looking at the range of sounds that can be produced and how sounds can be changed
- Try different ways of making sounds using the materials provided
- Make an instrument and use it to accompany singing
- Think about the characteristics of an animal and find a sound that expresses the characteristics.

Adult role
The adult will:

- Set up and introduce the display
- Replenish stocks of consumable resources daily
- Plan time to work alongside, and observe, children
- Intervene spontaneously as appropriate, asking questions and modelling use of key vocabulary.

Key vocabulary and questions
Vocabulary: Loud, quiet. Children should also be encouraged to use descriptive language, and make up their own words, related to sounds (e.g. 'rattling', 'banging', 'twanging', 'tinkling', 'pinging', 'swishing').
Questions: What kind of sound does the instrument make? Does it sound the same as this one? What kind of sound do you think this instrument will make? Can you find an instrument that makes a loud sound? Can you make an instrument that makes a rattling sound? What could you use to make a 'pinging' sound? Which instrument makes a sound like an elephant? What animal does this sound remind you of? Can you guess which instrument is making this sound?

When writing a plan, it is the content that is the important issue and, as long as the necessary information is included, the way in which it is organised and presented is a matter of preference. However, once the team has made a decision regarding format, it is helpful if all plans follow the chosen format.

The early years practitioner aims to encourage an independent approach to learning in young children and interactive display has an important role in encouraging both independent thought and independent use of resources. Young children's thinking can be challenged, and ideas developed, through stimulation of the imagination, exploration and investigation, and examples of displays included in this chapter illustrate a variety of 'starting points'. The way in which a display is arranged, labelled and used by adults will affect the way in which the child responds to it and interacts with it. For example, clear instructions, signs and labels, which are accompanied by pictures, photographs or symbols, will more easily enable a child to complete a task independently. An introduction to the display, including a verbal explanation and questions, focused on the learning objectives can also support the child in using the display independently – this introductory session could be planned as an adult focus in the weekly planning.

CASE STUDY

Leaf investigation

Type of display

- Wall/table top

Key areas of learning

- Knowledge and understanding of the world
- Communication, language and literacy

Learning objectives

- To observe and compare leaves, looking at shape, pattern and size
- To talk about observations
- To understand that non-fiction books can inform/to use non-fiction books as a source of information

Resources

- Photographs, posters, non-fiction picture books, children's drawings and paintings with a leaf/tree/autumn theme
- A range of autumn leaves
- Magnifying glasses
- Question cards, labels and key vocabulary cards

Suggested content of practitioner's introduction

- Look what we have on our book display today – what do you think the books are about? How do you know?
- Here are some of the leaves we collected in the park yesterday.
- Tell us what you already know about these leaves.
- Let's see what else we can find out about the leaves.
- Look closely at the leaves, what do you notice about them? Are they all the same colour/size? Can you see the patterns that the leaf 'veins' make?
- Look in the books. Look at the pictures. Can you match any of our leaves to the pictures? What kind of tree does this leaf come from? What happens to leaves in the autumn?

Following a brief introduction such as this, children are equipped with a purpose and appropriate resources for learning and should (although further adult input at a later stage will be helpful) be encouraged to carry out an independent 'leaf investigation'. Resources should also be made available for them to record their findings (e.g. mark-making equipment, bookmarks).

Of course, as with any learning activity, the practitioner must plan for differentiation and displays should be of interest and use to children at various developmental stages. In the example of the 'leaf investigation', the resources provided will enable learning to take place at all levels from, for example, tactile explorations with no verbal observations, to the accessing of information about specific leaves through reading pictures and key words.

CASE STUDY

Come and make a rocket

Figure 5.3 shows a display constructed in a setting attended by children throughout the foundation stage. It is a good example of a 'differentiated' display. The examples of 'possible activities' indicate the wide range of learning experiences that could take place on the 'journey' towards the early learning goals, particularly in the areas of knowledge and understanding of the world, and communication, language and literacy. The display enables children to begin the journey at their own starting point – it can challenge all children, but will exclude none.

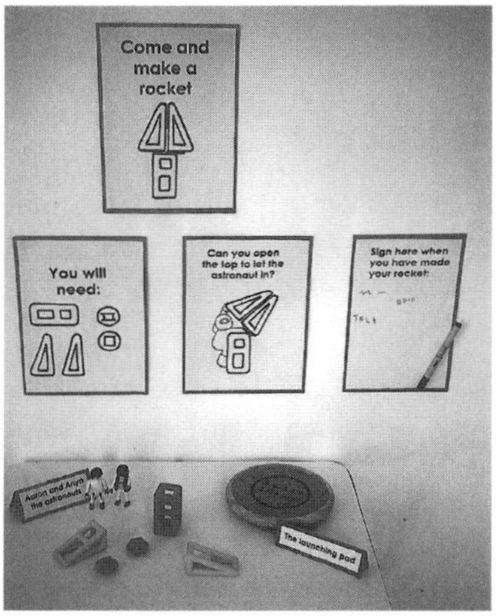

Figure 5.3 Come and make a rocket

Type of display

- Wall/table top

Key area of learning

- Knowledge and understanding of the world

Resources

- Signs (writing and diagrams): 'Come and make a rocket', 'You will need', 'Can you open the top to let the astronaut in?', 'Sign here when you have made your rocket'
- Components, 'astronaut' dolls, 'launching pad', pen

Possible activities

- Handling, looking at, comparing and talking about the components
- Experimenting with the components, finding ways of fixing them together
- Looking at the joined components and deciding what the 'model' could be (e.g. 'It looks like a tower!')
- Matching components to those on the 'You will need' sign

- Following the plan to build a rocket using the components[2]
- Exploring different ways of 'hinging' the top of the rocket
- Using the rocket in imaginative play or story-making activities
- Designing and making own rocket, talking about/recording plans or instructions (the child would need access to a range of components)
- Signing name (at own developmental stage of writing) to register engagement in the activity

CASE STUDY

Follow the blue arrows to find Blue Teddy's den

Children may be required to move around the setting in order to achieve objectives and displays could 'send' children on searches for objects or quests for information, perhaps following arrows or other signs. This example of this approach is an interesting variation on the traditional 'colour display', in this case, blue.

Type of display

- Table top (also requires children to move around the setting)

Key area of learning

- Mathematical development

Resources

- Table top: cards (displaying pictures of blue objects), large blue tray (for the collection of blue objects), colour vocabulary labels ('blue' label on tray), books and pictures about colour
- Blue arrows on walls leading to 'Blue Teddy's Den' – a den draped with lengths of blue fabric
- Inside the den: Blue Teddy, blue objects

Activity

Children take a picture card from the display showing a blue object (e.g. a blue ball), follow the blue arrows to Blue Teddy's den in the outside area, find the object (which will have been hidden by the practitioner in the den with other blue objects) and return it to the blue tray on the display. As children collect the blue objects, so the 'blue display' grows.

Activities such as this will be fun, and will, in addition to achieving the main objective of developing an understanding of 'blue', develop early reading and geographical skills. Children will 'read' the signs and clue cards as, for example, an adult would read road directions and road signs, to inform themselves about the location of their destination and to follow a route.

---

[2]   The display photographed offered a limited range of components (i.e. only those needed to build the rocket). Practitioners may decide to offer a wider range of components, requiring children to make the necessary selection when following the plan.

Looking at homes

Displays that are 'added to' by children are not exclusively collections as described in the previous example. They can also result in a collaborative piece of work such as a construction, as in the next example.

Type of display

- Table top/wall

Key area of learning

- Knowledge and understanding of the world

Resources

- Close-up photographs of brick and stone walls, photographs of builders at work
- Pictures of homes (semi-detached, terraced, detached houses, caravans, flats, bungalows, homes from other countries), copies of architects' plans, books about animals' homes, etc.
- 'Challenge card': 'Can you build a house for Robina? (small doll)
- Large selection of interlocking bricks

Activity

Children look at and talk about photographs and plans and build a house for a small doll using interlocking bricks. Individuals contribute to the building of the house over a period of time to produce a finished piece of work.

As well as offering information to children, the display will have engaged them in the practical application of their knowledge about building, given them an opportunity to practise a skill (joining bricks) and given them a purpose for building. Working with others on the construction will encourage evaluative discussion.

The question table

Parents can be involved in learning experiences with their child through interactive display and the 'question table' is a popular and effective example of such a display (Figure 5.4). It is often offered on a daily basis and can become part of the permanent provision. Children, supported by parents, are required as part of the beginning-of-session routine to

Figure 5.4 The Question Table

register their response to a daily question by placing their name card in a 'yes' or 'no' container.[3] The questions may refer to, for example, interests in the setting, or seasonal changes, or may aim to develop concepts. Children may be asked to:

- Observe
- Reason
- Recall
- Compare
- Predict
- Express opinions and preferences.

Although the name 'question table' implies a 'table-top' type of display, this activity could be just as successfully presented on a wall. For example, name cards in the shape of apples, and with self-adhesive hook-and-loop fastening tape attached to the back, could be removed from a wall-mounted carpet tile and displayed on either the 'yes' or the 'no' apple tree.

Listed below are some examples of questions:

- Did you pass a shop on your way to nursery today?
- Have the leaves started to fall off the trees yet?
- Are you wearing anything red today?
- Did you enjoy our 'dragon dance' yesterday?
- Is the ball in the box? (provide real objects)
- In our story yesterday, did the fox catch Rosie?
- Do you like to eat apples?
- Do you think it will rain today?
- Have you looked at our 'book of the week'?
- Have you got blue eyes? (provide a mirror)

A variation on the question-table idea is the 'question book'. This is usually a large scrapbook covered in 'special' paper. The question is written at the top of the page, and children respond by signing their name in the 'yes' column or the 'no' column. It can be interesting for children to look back at previous pages with an adult, and compare responses to questions.

OTHER EXAMPLES OF INTERACTIVE DISPLAY

'Owl Babies' behaviour chart

Type of display

- Wall/suspended

Key area of learning

- Personal, social and emotional development

---

[3] This does not always have to be the case – children could be offered a number of alternative answers, e.g. 'What is your favourite colour?' Children are required to put their name card in the red, blue or yellow bowl (labelled with colour names). Practitioners should take care not to confuse children by frequently changing the 'answering system'.

Working towards key QCA early learning goal

- Work as part of a group or class, taking turns and sharing fairly, understanding that there need to be agreed values and codes of behaviour for groups of people, including adults and children, to work together harmoniously.

Resources

- Setting's 'rules' sign (e.g. 'Be kind to other children and look after our toys')
- Large picture of an owl, tree pictures and a picture of three baby owls – pictures to be cut out, laminated and arranged vertically or horizontally (large owl, trees, baby owls)
- Sign: 'I want my Mummy!'
- Book: *Owl Babies* by Martin Waddell

Activity

Children will be familiar with the *Owl Babies* story. They, as a group, move the 'Mummy' owl towards her babies (one tree at a time) in response to evidence that the rules are being adhered to. When Mummy owl reaches her babies, the whole group receives a 'reward', such as another visit from Oscar the clown (see chapter 4, p. 92).

Weaving a Christmas Tree

Type of display

- Table top

Key area of learning

- Creative development

Working towards key QCA early learning goal

- Explore colour, texture, shape, form and space in two and three dimensions.

Resources

- A willow twig 'wigwam'or large, triangular piece of plastic webbing (both available from garden centres – intended for training climbing plants)
- Box containing strips of green (a range of shades) fabric, ribbon and cord
- Key vocabulary labels (e.g. weave, over, under, in, out)

Activity

Children, and parents, select pieces of fabric etc. to weave into the framework to create a 'woven Christmas tree' over a period of two to three weeks prior to Christmas. The tree can then be adorned with children's made decorations tied onto the framework.

Whose shoes?

Type of display

- Table top

Key area of learning

- Mathematical development

Working towards key QCA early learning goal

- Use language such as 'circle' or 'bigger' to describe the shape and size of solids and flat shapes.

Resources

- Five pairs of shoes (soles of various shapes and sizes), templates of the shoes arranged in pairs on the table top
- Key vocabulary labels (e.g. big, small)

Activity

Children match the shoes to the correct templates, looking carefully at size and shape.

Look how we have changed!

Type of display

- Wall

Key area of learning

- Knowledge and understanding of the world

Working towards key QCA early learning goal

- Find out about past and present events in their own lives, and in those of their families and other people they know.

Resources

- Folded cards attached to the wall – one for each child, showing a picture of the child as a baby on the front, and as they are now, inside
- Posters and pictures of 'babyhood'

Activity

Children guess who the baby photographs are, and then lift the flap to find out if they were correct. They talk about how they have changed in terms of appearance, food, independence, and so on.

Make a game

Type of display

- Table top/wall

Key area of learning

- Mathematical development (children can work towards all *early learning goals* for mathematical development during this activity)

Resources

- Large grid attached to table
- Photocopied grids and sheets of plain paper available in folders attached to wall
- Dice and spinners (numerals and colours)
- Small 'sorting' shapes (red, yellow and blue)
- Coloured crayons
- Number lines (1–10)

Activity

Children devise and play their own games and explain rules to their friends.

Where's Spot?

Type of display

- Table top

Key area of learning

- Mathematical development

Working towards key QCA early learning goal

- Use everyday words to describe position.

Resources

- Book: *Where's Spot?* by Eric Hill
- 'Spot' soft toy
- Photographs of Spot in different positions around the setting
- Question labels (e.g. Can you hide/find Spot under the table? On the cupboard? In the box? Under the chair?)

Activity

Children work with a friend, hiding and finding Spot, and using key 'positional' vocabulary to describe his location.

Five Little Speckled Frogs

Type of display

- Table top/wall

Key area of learning

- Mathematical development

Working towards key QCA early learning goal

- Count reliably up to ten everyday objects.

Resources

- Rhyme: '5 Little Speckled Frogs'
- Numerals 1–5
- Real log
- Five frog models
- Pond (e.g. small silver foil tray, tissue paper 'pond weed', small stones – children could make this)

Activity

Children sing the rhyme, counting the frogs and putting them into the pool in turn.

Story characters

Type of display

- Table top/suspended

Key area of learning

- Communication, language and literacy

Working towards key QCA early learning goal

- Show an understanding of the elements of stories, such as main character, sequence of events, and openings, and how information can be found in non-fiction texts to answer questions about where, who, why and how.

Resources

- Silhouettes of familiar story-book characters (e.g. Kipper, the monster from *Not Now Bernard*, Big Bear and Little Bear from *Let's Go Home Little Bear*) cut out of black sugar paper, laminated for durability and hung at different levels from a length of dowel suspended above the table top
- All corresponding books displayed on the table top

ity

...ren recognise and talk about the characters and match silhouettes to pictures in books.

Display can celebrate

Display can be used to celebrate:

- Children's achievements
- Adults' work (e.g. artists)
- Different cultures, languages, beliefs, interests and experiences.

Using display for the purpose of celebration can promote learning in the area of personal, social and emotional development by helping to:

- Raise self-esteem
- Develop in children a respect for own work and the work of others
- Develop in children respect for, and understanding of, different cultures and beliefs.

Celebration of children's work is a reason for display with which most practitioners feel comfortable. Traditionally the display of children's art work has become a characteristic feature of the early years setting. Of course it is important to value and celebrate work of this nature, but in doing so practitioners should not exclude work in other areas of the curriculum. Children's achievements in all areas of learning should be in evidence in the setting, and unique qualities and individuality recognised.

In selecting work for display, the practitioner should consider the achievements of the individual, and not judge all work against an inflexible standard in order to display the 'best' items. Although work of a high standard should indeed be displayed, and those children applauded for their achievements, it should not exclude, or undermine, the achievements of those at an earlier stage on the 'learning journey'.

When displaying children's work, the practitioner may choose to exhibit only the finished piece of work or may decide to show the process, or contributory work. A series of photographs of work in progress (e.g. models made in the workshop) is an effective way of showing how the child has arrived at the 'end product'. This type of display will not only serve as a teaching aid to other children, but will also communicate the message to children and adults that the learning process is as important as the end result. The photographic display is also a good way of celebrating learning achievements that produce no concrete, or permanent, evidence, such as investigating snow in the water tray, mark-making with water and brushes in the outside area (see Figure 1.14, p. 34) and shadow play (see Figure 1.15, p. 36).

In the case of observational drawing or painting, it is a good idea, where possible, to display the stimulus alongside children's work. This will encourage further observation and discussion.

Activities planned around a theme will often generate some exciting work for display. During a focus on 'hats', for example, activities may be as diverse as trying on different hats and looking at themselves in a mirror, drawing themselves in hats from observation, making up stories about a bejewelled crown, decorating straw hats, and making hats in the workshop to support role play. A display of children's work showing one aspect of this project could be constructed, or the 'one aspect' could be displayed in the context of all the other related learning.

Following the 'Jungle Play' and 'Lion's Visit' focus activities described in chapter 3, a display was constructed that incorporated the following:

- Photographs of 'jungle environments' built by children in the construction area
- Children's paintings of Lion
- Photographs of children constructing dens for Lion in the outside play area and the construction area
- Photographs of the finished den constructions with the lion 'in residence'
- Children's records of materials used to build the dens (picture tick lists, drawings, attempts at written lists)
- Children's letters to Lion
- Photographs of musical instruments made (spontaneously by children in the workshop) for Lion to play in his den
- Children's records of whether their musical instrument produced a 'loud' or 'quiet' sound.

This display also included:

- Lion in his 'jungle box' and letters from Lion (see Figures 3.1 and 3.2) to the children (the stimulus for 'Lion's Visit')
- A list of pertinent early learning goals.

More general celebrations showing the range of activities in which children engage across all areas of provision will generate interest from parents and children, and can be quite enlightening to visitors. Figure 5.5 is an example of such a display. Content includes paintings, writing for different purposes, drawings, three-dimensional work, photographs of children working in areas of provision and brief explanations written by the practitioner.

Children's achievements can also be celebrated on audio tape and a suitable tape recorder included on a table-top display. 'Sound' poems (e.g. water sounds), word poems, singing, children making music and children talking about holiday experiences or favourite toys can easily be taped and children will enjoy listening.

Figure 5.5 Look what we do in Nursery

Areas of provision such as the workshop and construction area should offer permanent display provision for the celebration of children's work and often the most practical type of display is the open shelf (Figure 5.6). The content of such display may be of a transient nature but it is important that children have a 'safe' place to put their work, either while it is in progress or when it is finished. Children will learn to value their own work and that of others, and will enjoy looking at and talking about 'exhibits'. Folded cards and pencils should be supplied in order for children to make name labels to display next to their work.

Figure 5.6 Displaying children's work in the construction area

Part of the practitioner's role as an educator is to model skills and it is sometimes appropriate to include the work of adults in a display, preferably alongside the work of the children, thereby giving equal status to both. This could be a model made in the setting by a parent, a carving by a local craftsperson, a letter written to the children by a member of staff, a photograph of a parent playing football for the local team or a reproduction of a painting by a famous artist.

An awareness of, and respect for, the beliefs and cultures of others should be part of the very fabric of the curriculum. Display should both reflect the attitude of respect and celebrate cultural diversity. The artefacts used should always be of good quality and authentic, and the information accurate. Parents and other members of the community will often be happy to share traditions and help with the writing of dual-language signs.

Acquaint children with cross cultural symbols by collecting and displaying images of the sun, trees, birds and so on from various cultures and by talking about the moods the different images evoke. Does this bird look strong? Gentle? Helpful?

(Chapman 1978)

This section concludes with several other examples of display for celebration:

Meet the authors

Type of display

- Table top/wall

Key area of learning

- Communication, language and literacy

Content

- Books by familiar authors (e.g. Eric Carle, Mick Inkpen, Pat Hutchins), photographs and brief biographical sketch of each
- Book reviews by children and their parents
- Examples of books of children's work compiled by the practitioner
- Examples of children's story-making/writing attempts, with photographs and brief biographical sketches of them

Celebrating

- Children as authors

The magic tree

Type of display

- Table top (workshop)

Key area of learning

- Knowledge and understanding of the world

Content

- A branch secured in a pot of sand to look like a tree
- Children's work (e.g. magic jewels, made jewellery, Christmas tree decorations) displayed hanging on the branch

Celebrating

- Children's skills (design and technology) and imaginative ideas

The Gallery[3]

Type of display

- Wall

---

[3]   The 'gallery' idea can also be used to display 3D work.

Key area of learning

- Creative development

Content

- Children's paintings, prints, drawings and collages displayed alongside the work of established artists from different times and cultures

Celebrating

- Children as artists

The 'action' mobile

Type of display

- Suspended

Key area of learning

- Physical development

Content

Photographs (pairs stuck together, back to back) of children (climbing, balancing, running, hopping, throwing/catching/kicking balls, crawling through tubes, riding bikes and scooters, sliding down the slide) hanging on threads (at different levels) and suspended from a wire frame, or from branches of a tree in the outside area.

Celebrating

- Children's physical achievements (large motor skills)

The window hanging

Type of display

- Suspended

Key area of learning

- Creative development

Content

Children's tissue paper collages on acetate sheet, joined together (by treasury tags threaded through holes at the top and bottom of each collage) and hung in front of a window.

Celebrating

- Children's creative expression

Display can be informative

Most aspects of displays have now been covered in this chapter but guidance would not be complete without highlighting the purpose of display in communicating information. This reason for display has already been included as an aspect of other types of display, but there are cases when the main purpose of a display is to inform.

Display can be used to inform:

- Children
- Adults working in the setting
- Parents.

The type of information displayed will vary but, in general terms, can be divided into the following areas:

- Information that directly supports the child in the learning process, either through factual content or instruction
- Information that helps the adult to support the child's learning
- Information that helps the adult to understand curricular aims and the nature of children's learning
- Practical information related to the organisation of the setting.

Direct support can include the provision of books, posters, pictures and photographs to support a learning focus. For example, during a 'topic' on water, the practitioner may construct a wall display in the water area which informs the child about various uses of water. This could include photographs of children using water in the setting for a variety of purposes (e.g. drinking, bathing dolls, washing paint brushes, mixing paints, pouring from teapots during tea parties, washing hands, watering plants). Posters and photographs of water being used outside the setting could also be displayed (e.g. swimming pools, car washes, agricultural watering systems, narrow boats transporting people on canals, window cleaners).

'Topic' work can also be supported by table-top displays offering information in the form of artefacts such as bowls, plates, cups and cutlery made from different materials, and originating from different cultures, during a focus on 'food'. Many local authorities have a central stock of artefacts from which practitioners are able to select and borrow. Of course, it is best, where possible, to allow children to handle artefacts, but it may be that some of the 'exhibits' are quite fragile and unlikely to stand up to constant handling. In this case they will have to be protected (perhaps in a plastic case) and children taught to look carefully. If practitioners wish the display to be 'interactive', children could be offered the necessary resources and encouraged to draw objects from observation.

Displays can also inform children about, and instruct them how to use, equipment in an area of provision. In, for example, the painting area a display could be constructed to show children the routines, tools and materials involved in mixing powder paint, as in the following example.

Mixing paint

(In order for children to access the information independently, instructions should be illustrated with clear drawings or photographs.)

- Put on a red apron.
- Collect a palette, paint pots, water pot, spatula.
- Take your water pot to the tap and fill it with water.
- Choose a piece of paper and a brush.
- Use the spatula to put some powder paint in the palette.
- Use the brush to mix the paint with water.

Now you are ready to paint.

This sort of information displayed in the setting is also very useful to adults in supporting children. When all adults encourage children to follow the same routines, these routines will become established quickly, and children will soon feel confident in using equipment independently.

Displaying information about curricular aims helps parents and other adults in the setting to understand how and why learning takes place. Such information can be displayed alongside other displays in explanation of activities or learning experiences, or can be sited in an area of provision giving examples, and aims, of cross-curricular learning. It will probably include reference to the key area of learning and early learning goals.

Constructing displays: some practical hints

The following hints are of a practical nature and may be useful to practitioners when constructing displays.

Wall display

- A simple, 'uncluttered' display is usually effective and easy to 'read'. The temptation to cram too much onto the board should be resisted – the result will probably be visual chaos and confusion for the children.
- Coloured work should be mounted carefully. Unless all the work has a common colour theme and can be unified by one colour (e.g. autumn leaves: orange), brightly coloured mounts and backing paper should be avoided as they will detract from, or conflict with, the displayed work. Black-and-white work such as pencil or charcoal drawings can more effectively be mounted on a bright colour.
- The mount should be kept fairly narrow; it is rarely necessary to exceed 1 cm. A slightly wider mount at the bottom will prevent the illusion of the work 'slipping' down.
- All lines should be straight. The composition of a display can be helped by the lining up of verticals and horizontals.

- Arranging items selected for display on the floor before attaching them to the wall is often a useful exercise. It will be easy to move them around until a final decision has been made.
- The composition of a child's work should not be altered by cutting away large amounts.
- To add another dimension to the wall board, a shelf can be attached. This can be used to display items such as books, toys and natural forms. Shelves can easily be made from strong cardboard boxes (see Figure 5.7). They can then be painted or covered with paper or fabric. Once stapled to the wall, the 'box shelves' should provide a firm surface although it is not advisable to display anything too heavy on them. (Shelves must be visually accessible to children).

Figure 5.7 Making a shelf for a wall display

Table top display

- Wooden blocks or upturned boxes under draped fabric are effective in creating surfaces for display at different levels.
- Plywood cuboids (a range of sizes) painted in white emulsion can be used to display natural forms in a simple but eye-catching way.
- Free-standing labels can be made from folded card or signs and labels can be displayed in moulded perspex photograph frames.
- A covering of hessian can be an effective surface on which to display natural forms.

Shelf display

- Open 'grid' shelving units attached to the wall, mounted on unbreakable mirror sheets, make an interesting display. Items will be reflected in the mirror, giving the impression of another dimension, and children will be offered an alternative view of the items.
- Grid shelving units painted with matt, black paint show off white objects effectively and create a striking display.
- Shelves attached to adjustable brackets slotted into aluminium strips (all widely available in DIY stores) on the wall make a versatile structure for display. The height of the spaces between shelves can be altered, and shelves removed if necessary.
- Wide shelves (at least 30 cm) are necessary in the workshop area to avoid the frustration of larger models falling off.
- When space is limited, shelves can be hinged and folded flat to the wall when not in use.

)ended display

If a number of items are being displayed, they should hang at different levels and not obscure other items or displays from children's vision.

- Hanging items are constantly twisting and turning and may be more effective if double sided. This point is particularly applicable to hanging word labels.
- Practitioners should check that the display is not going to obstruct adults or children (or interfere with 'beamed' security systems!), and should guard against an 'oppressive' feeling in the setting resulting from too much material hanging from low ceilings.
- The effect of transparent or 'sparkly' displays will probably be enhanced if they are situated close to a light source.

Through trial and error, and through the sharing of practice between colleagues, the practitioner will build up a bank of ideas for display, which can be adapted and combined to suit the needs of the children and characteristics of the setting. The examples given in this chapter are a small sample but show how display can, with a little imagination and planning, make an exciting contribution to the environment, inspiring children to *want* to learn and equipping them with the necessary tools and information to support them in their learning.

Curiosity and intrinsic motivation are closely linked and there is no doubt they play an important part in helping children to develop positive attitudes towards learning. One of the main functions of the nursery is to provide a stimulating, enriching environment where children are encouraged to 'learn how to learn'.

(Curtis 1998)

CHAPTER 6

Observing children's play, assessing learning and keeping useful records

Assessment gives insight into children's interests, and possible difficulties in their learning from which next steps in learning and teaching can be planned.

(QCA 2000)

The content of this chapter is organised as follows:

- The assessment and planning cycle (p. 127)
- Collecting information during the 'first contact' period (p. 128)
- Observation and assessment in the setting (p. 129)
- Recording and reporting (p. 137)

The assessment and planning cycle

Observation, assessment and planning are all vital aspects of the educator's role and part of an on-going cycle of identifying and providing for children's learning needs. Figure 6.1 explains this cycle and shows clearly how one stage informs the next.

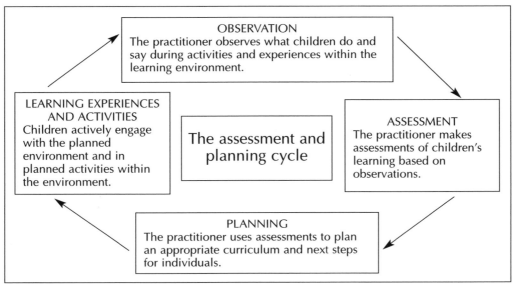

Figure 6.1 The assessment and planning cycle

Collecting information during the 'first contact' period

Neither the learning process nor the 'assessment cycle' begin as the child enters the setting – parents have already spent three years with their child, observing and supporting his or her diverse learning, and will have assimilated a wealth of useful information. A child's learning will be continued, and built upon, in the setting. Prior experiences and achievements will influence the way in which a child approaches a new learning situation, and will impact on the learning that takes place. Practitioners should encourage parents to share information about their child on entry, and throughout their time at the setting.

In chapter 4, ways in which useful information can be communicated between practitioner and parents were suggested. Ideas include the use of forms and questionnaires (during the 'first contact' period) on which to record personal details and also information about the child's previous experiences. The practitioner may complete the form during discussion with the parent or, alternatively, parents may be asked to complete it at their own convenience. Recorded information could include:

- Full name, date of birth, address and telephone number
- Names of main carers and siblings
- Home language
- Religion
- Contact names, addresses and telephone numbers
- Health – details of any contact with specialists or other agencies
- Previous preschool experience (response re: settling in, relationships with other children, activities enjoyed)
- Significant experiences such as a new baby in the family, loss of a family member, house move
- Particular interests
- Skill development e.g. using the toilet, dressing self, riding a tricycle, using tools (e.g. cutlery, a pencil)
- Any anxieties or behaviour issues.

Many practitioners also produce an 'About Me' booklet, which parent and child are encouraged to complete together at home. The child is often asked to bring the booklet back to the setting in order for the practitioner to talk with him or her about the content. It can then be included in the child's records. The 'About Me' booklet will probably require the adult and child to respond to statements such as the following:

- This is me. My name is
- I am _____ years old.
- I live with
- My pets are
- My friends are
- My favourite book is
- My favourite toy is
- My favourite food is
- I am happy when
- When I come to preschool, I will play with

Ample space should be available in each section for child's mark-making.

Some of the information collected at this early stage will mainly be of practical use to staff and some will be more directly useful in planning the curriculum for the child. A composite of all the information will help to give practitioners an understanding of where the child is on the 'learning journey', and provide a bank of knowledge that will enable the adult to interact more productively with the child.

During the period of first contact, information about the child can be acquired through observation of responses during, for example, the home visit, as this practitioner's account illustrates:

As we arrived at the house for the home visit, Alistair flung open the door and shouted excitedly to his Gran: 'My teachers are here!' He was eager to look at the nursery photograph album and asked questions about the activities, particularly those taking place in the outside area. When asked if he liked to play outside, he responded 'Yes – I like to ride my bike – I want to go on that bike' (pointing to the nursery tandem bike in the photograph). Alistair showed us his train track with pride and explained how he had fixed it together – Gran says that he spends a lot of time playing with his train, looking in his train books and watching his train video. As I talked with Gran, Stella (other member of staff) joined in the 'train play'. After a short while, Alistair's cousin (present during the whole visit) approached and asked to play. The two children became quite engrossed for about 10 minutes taking turns in pushing the train around the track to the shops, park, etc. At the end of the visit, I explained to Alistair that I had to go back to nursery and would see him again when he next came to nursery, and he replied 'Can I come back with you now?'.

The account tells staff the following information, which can then be used, in conjunction with other information, when planning Alistair's 'settling-in' programme:

- He uses spoken language readily.
- He is interested in what happens in nursery.
- He is eager to come to nursery.
- He is keen to play outside.
- He likes to ride bikes.
- He is interested in trains.
- He is able to maintain concentration at a self-chosen activity.
- He is able to share and take turns with another child.
- He approaches adults with confidence in familiar surroundings.

Observation and assessment in the setting

Victoria Hurst and Margaret Lally comment that:

Children tell us about themselves through their behaviour, and there are clues to how we can best teach them to be found in their play and social interactions, in their conversations and the things they bring to school, in the way they use opportunities to explore new areas of learning and in the way they create stories, pictures, models and music.

(Hurst and Lally 1992)

Observing children's play is the key to understanding their interests and learning needs and is a salient feature of the 'teaching' role. Practitioners will need to allow time for observation of children at play in the setting. Such 'observation time' may be pre-planned, with a definite focus, or may be incidental. Observations can be written down, or noted verbally, but however they are reported, practitioners should have an effective system for sharing observations. A brief, daily meeting when staff talk about their observations of children can be a successful way of 'pooling' information, as can regular entries in, and discussion of, children's profiles (see pp. 138–143).

The broad aim of observation is:

- To gather information that will enable the practitioner to assess children's learning and consequently plan an appropriate curriculum, providing for the full range of needs within the setting.

More particularly, practitioners may decide to make focused observations with the ultimate aim of:

- Assessing the learning of individuals, identifying needs and planning 'next steps' for individuals and groups of children (such observations may focus on an area of learning, or one aspect of an area)
- Evaluating and improving areas of provision in terms of learning opportunities for all children
- Raising the profile of an area of learning and ensuring that learning in this area is taking place for all children and throughout the setting.

Observing and assessing individuals

Practitioners observe children in order to find out:

- What they are able to do (skills)
- What they know and understand (knowledge and concepts)
- How they approach learning (attitudes).

When observing individuals, the practitioner may 'track' a child over a period of time, perhaps looking specifically at an area of development. Alternatively, the child may be observed in a particular area of provision or during a focus activity. Sometimes a child is 'targeted' by the team, and all practitioners make observations as they come into contact with him or her over the course of a session, or a few sessions. Although it is essential to plan observations such as those just described, the necessity for practitioners to be constantly 'tuned in' to children's learning should be stressed. Opportunities to observe and assess should be taken as they arise. Quite often unplanned observations are made in response to a significant behaviour or activity, and these can provide just as useful information as the 'scheduled' observations.

Young children should not be put in a 'test' situation. Assessment should always take place in an appropriate context and, when a practitioner decides to plan an activity in order to assess certain aspects of a child's learning, that activity must be purposeful and interesting to the child.

When making structured observations, it can be useful to refer to lists of statements or questions; these prompts will help the practitioner to focus observations and to make clear assessments. In the following example, the practitioner had planned, in the weekly planning, to observe new children during the settling-in period, and started with the questions:

- *Who* do I want to observe?
- *What* do I want to find out about the child?
- *How* will I find out that information?
- *How* will I use the information?

CASE STUDY

Observation of Natasha

I want to assess Natasha's social development (particularly relationships with other children and participation in group play), and to know where she is on her journey towards the following early learning goals:

- Form good relationships with adults and peers
- Work as part of a group or class, taking turns and sharing fairly, understanding that there need to be agreed values and codes of behaviour for groups of people, including adults and children, to work together harmoniously.

(Personal, social and emotional development)

I will track her throughout the setting for 10-minute observation periods on Monday, Wednesday and Friday. I will use the assessment to inform future planning of Natasha's learning in the area of social development.

The practitioner then observed Natasha, bearing in mind the following questions. Does she:

- Observe other children's play from a 'safe' distance?
- Work alone in an area of provision?
- Work alongside other children, but with no interaction?
- Attempt contact with other children in close proximity (e.g. making eye contact or offering toys)?
- Interact with other children during play (e.g. through conversation about the activity, giving and receiving objects)?
- Take turns and share?
- Work cooperatively with other children, negotiating and problem solving?

At the end of the week, the practitioner had collected the following information:

Monday: Natasha spent 10 minutes in the home corner. At first she 'hovered' in the doorway watching as Tom and Lindsey set the table and pretended to eat tea. The other two children then left the area and Natasha sat at the table, rearranged the plates and cups and pretended to drink. As others entered and left the area she continued her play at the table.

Wednesday: Natasha played (briefly) alone in the sand area filling containers left by other children. She then moved to the office (again, no children in the area) and began mark-making. Andrew entered and sat down at the table with her. She looked up and watched as he selected a pencil and some paper. Andrew asked Natasha if she would like a pencil, she shook her head, looked down and continued with her mark-making. After five minutes in the office, Natasha observed (for two or three minutes) two children playing in the water area and then wandered outside.

Friday: Natasha approached the workshop where three children were already working. She watched from a distance of half a metre until Mrs Dent encouraged her to put on an apron, select some materials and make a model. After a little more support from Mrs Dent re: appropriate use of tools, Natasha worked happily alongside the other children, pausing occasionally to observe what they were doing. When Sally explained to her that she had made a model of a dinosaur, Natasha looked at her face, and although there was no verbal response, eye contact was made.

The practitioner analysed the information collected during the observations to make an assessment of her learning:

Assessment: Natasha does spend time observing other children's play and quite often engages in solitary play in an area. She can be reluctant to enter an area of provision if others are already working in the area. However, she is happy to work alongside other children if they enter the area after her, or if an adult supports her in entering the group and engaging in play. She is beginning to communicate with other children by non-verbal means, and to respond to their approaches.

The assessment of Natasha's social development was then used to plan her next steps in that area of learning.

Next steps

- To choose to work alongside other children more frequently and to gain confidence in entering an area in which other children are already working
- To develop non-verbal contact with other children (e.g. passing objects, smiling), and to begin to respond verbally

Planned experiences/activities

Adult input:

Support Natasha in entering an area of provision already being used by other children. Teach/reinforce routines and appropriate use of equipment in each area. Spend time playing in areas of provision with groups of children (including Natasha), encouraging interaction between children.

Focus activities:

- Teddy bears' tea party in the home corner – setting the table for children and bears, passing food to each guest, pouring tea for everyone
- Circle games: rolling the ball to a friend (saying the friend's name before rolling), passing the teddy around the circle, pass the smile around the circle (each child, in turn, smiles at the child sitting next to them)
- Making presents/writing letters and giving them to a friend

Of course, what the practitioner learnt about Natasha during the periods of observation will not have been restricted to the area of social development targeted. Other useful information will have been gleaned. For example, the practitioner will probably have been enlightened about Natasha's mathematical development from watching her filling containers with sand on Wednesday. Such information can be valuable to the practitioner in planning for other areas of learning, and its contribution to the whole picture of a child's learning development should not be disregarded. When making focused observations, the skill is in registering the 'additional' information, without being distracted from the focus of the observation.

Making assessments of individuals from a number of observations (focused or incidental) over a period of time, rather than from one isolated observation, will give a more accurate picture of a child's stage of development, revealing strands and patterns across a range of situations. Sometimes patterns in children's play (interests, preoccupations or repeated behaviours) become apparent and form the basis of planning for individuals. For example, a child might be observed joining paper clips together with treasury tags, playing with interlocking jigsaws, connecting components from a construction set, and taping together cardboard tubes. Such observations would indicate to the practitioner that the child is fascinated by 'connection' and may prompt her to offer the child a range of materials and equipment through which to explore this perception further.

The importance of matching the curriculum to the child has already been highlighted a number of times in previous chapters on planning but cannot be over-emphasised. It is as a result of observing and assessing individuals that the practitioner is able to define and address their needs. With sound assessment procedures in place, staff will be able to identify any special educational needs at an early stage, and produce effective Individual Education Plans (IEPs) to support children in making progress.[1]

In order to plan appropriately for the child's next steps, the practitioner needs to be aware of the stages that a child passes through on the journey towards, and beyond, the early learning goals. Some practitioners will have studied children's development in areas of learning during their initial training and perhaps through subsequent training, others may feel less confident in this area. The DfEE guidance material in *Curriculum Guidance for the Foundation Stage* (QCA 2000) for practitioners in early years settings offers examples of children working at different stages and breaks down learning (in each curricular area) into 'stepping stones'. Practitioners will probably find the guidance a helpful tool in understanding children's learning and in planning 'next steps'. Some Baseline Assessment frameworks also offer a useful 'breakdown' of children's learning and LEAs will be able to advise practitioners on an appropriate framework.

As the practitioner observes children, it may become apparent that a few have reached a similar stage in their development and are ready for certain next steps at the same time, or that two or three children have a shared interest. It may then be appropriate to plan an activity (or series of activities) for this group.

---

[1] *Curriculum Guidance for the Foundation Stage* (QCA 2000) states that 'from September 2001, it is anticipated that the revised SEN Code of Practice will specify particular requirements for intervention in early years settings'.

Evaluating and improving the provision

In aiming to offer all children rich learning opportunities in areas of provision, practitioners will have produced long-term plans detailing key areas of learning, resources, organisation, anticipated learning experiences/activities, adult role and key questions/vocabulary (see chapter 1). Regular observation of children's play in each area will provide teams with the necessary information to evaluate the success of the area in terms of children's learning, to review long-term plans and to make the necessary changes to improve provision.

Before spending time observing in an area of provision, it will probably be a good idea to read through the long-term plan for that area. Asking the following questions while observing in an area is also likely to be helpful:

- Which children are choosing to work in the area?
- Are all needs being met? (Taking into consideration: gender, special educational needs, disabilities, more able children, ethnic groups and religious, social and cultural backgrounds)
- Which resources are being used? (frequently? regularly? occasionally? never?)
- How are children using the resources?
- How are all areas of learning developed through the provision? Which are the dominant areas?
- What kind of activities/learning experiences are taking place?
- What have the children learnt?

Figure 6.2 illustrates how observations of children in the water area have been used by the practitioner, or team of practitioners, to:

- Plan possible follow-up activities and next steps for individuals
- Assess provision in the water area.[2]

In order to check that there is breadth and balance in the curriculum, practitioners will need to study assessments of provision and this is one of the reasons for keeping clear records (see below, 'Recording and reporting'). As identified in the long-term plans, each area of provision will promote 'key' areas of learning (although learning will not be exclusive to these areas). An overview of assessment records for each area of provision will inform the practitioner as to how successfully the long-term aims are being met in practice. Discussion of these records by the team should then lead to any necessary changes being made.

Assessing how areas of learning are being developed in the setting

Practitioners can assess how a particular area of learning, or aspect of an area, is being developed throughout the setting using a similar procedure to that used in evaluating provision. Children will be observed in all areas of provision and with a focus on, for example, writing. The practitioner will look at the purposes for writing and opportunities to write that children are offered, and also at the provision of mark-making equipment and how this is used. The data collected from observations will then be collated and used to inform long-term planning.

---

[2] Other observations of children's use of water provision (made over a period of four weeks) were also considered as the team discussed implications for the future – it is advisable to make a series of observations when assessing provision in order to be sure that the full picture is reflected.

DATE: 10, 14 June		TIME/DURATION: 9.30am/15 minutes each day
CHILD	ACTIVITY	POSSIBLE NEXT STEPS FOR THE CHILD/FOLLOW-UP ACTIVITIES
Tamara	Lining up plastic bottles on the side of the tray, randomly selected from the shelf. Picking up bottles, one at a time, putting them down again.	Counting experience and familiarity with number language, particularly number names 1–5. Plan opportunities for counting in a 'real' context.
	Filling plastic bottles with water (using jugs) and then emptying them.	More 'filling/emptying' activities using various containers, perhaps in dry sand or home corner (tea parties). Understanding/using vocabulary: full/empty.
Shelley and Patrick	Playing with boats. Filling boats with water and watching them sink.	Finding out how many plastic pots full of water can be poured into the boat before it sinks. Further investigation: floating and sinking using a range of materials and objects. Making own boats. Understanding/using key vocabulary, float, sink.
	'Story-making' about boats in a shark-infested sea.	Opportunities for developing story ideas and sharing them with other children.
Sean	Using water poured from plastic bottles to make the water wheel work.	Making water wheels using e.g. plastic spoons. Looking at other ways of moving objects using water.
Kelly-Marie, Holly, Jordan	Using plastic containers, first child fills up a container, passes it to the next child who passes it to the third child who empties it into a transparent plastic bottle. Holly asked 'Is it full – put some more in?' and when it was full, said 'Now make it empty'. The other children responded appropriately.	Counting how many containers full of water it takes to fill a jug, bowl, bucket, etc. Comparing containers re: capacity. Vocabulary: Kelly-Marie, Jordan: Confident use of full/empty, understand and begin to use comparative vocabulary e.g. more, less, fuller. Holly – use increased range of comparative vocabulary with confidence. Develop 'chain gang' cooperative work, e.g. 'Can you pass the cup of water along a chain of 5 children without spilling any?' – negotiation of roles.
	Making ice creams using yoghurt pots. 'Selling' ice creams.	Hot/cold, freezing/melting investigations in the water tray, making real ice lollies. Ice-cream van role play.
Tim	Watching Kelly-Marie, Holly and Jordan's play.	Encouragement to join in play with other children and to become physically involved with resources in exploration and investigation.

GENERAL OBSERVATIONS:

- Children tend to leave equipment in the water tray when they move away from the area. This is inhibiting other children's play and discouraging some from entering the area.
- Most verbal interaction took place during imaginative play.
- Little attention was paid to pictures and photographs displayed in the area.

Figure 6.2 Observation and assessment: The water area

OBSERVED LEARNING IN THE SIX AREAS OF LEARNING

COMMUNICATION, LANGUAGE AND LITERACY	MATHEMATICAL DEVELOPMENT
Giving verbal instructions to another child. Asking questions. Listening and taking turns in conversation. Use of descriptive language ('It's making a clapping noise like a waterfall'). Use of mathematical language (e.g. full, empty, more). Some reference to resources by name. 'Story-making' – discussion of characters and events. Signing name on 'register' on leaving the area.	Investigating capacity – filling /emptying. Early counting, and one-to-one counting of four children to four aprons. Use of mathematical language such as more, full, number names. Matching resources to templates, looking at shape and height. Matching numbers on resources to numbers on templates.

PERSONAL, SOCIAL AND EMOTIONAL DEVELOPMENT	KNOWLEDGE AND UNDERSTANDING OF THE WORLD
Working together – one child holding a container while another pours water into it; 'chain-gang' approach to passing resources. Child showing interest while observing others. Involvement in an activity. Concentration during an investigation. Independent selection and use of resources.	Investigating 'water power' (water wheels) and floating and sinking. Discussion of hot and cold in relation to ice creams. Understanding the water can make materials wet, and can 'spread' on a flat, non-absorbent surface (water spilt on clothing and floor).

CREATIVE DEVELOPMENT	PHYSICAL DEVELOPMENT
Story-making – using imagination and expressing ideas (boat/sharks story) Role play – making and selling ice creams	Coordination – Pouring from one container to another, holding a container in one hand and pouring water into it from a container in the other hand, passing containers to the next child in the line.

TEAM DISCUSSION: IMPLICATIONS FOR THE FUTURE/ACTION TO BE TAKEN:

- All staff to encourage children to replace resources before leaving the area. To ensure that provision is also supporting children in doing this, C.P. will renew templates, replace storage boxes for tubes, shells, stones, yoghurt pots, etc. with shallow baskets and label these clearly with pictures and words.

- Plan 'link' activities between areas (e.g. making water wheels in the workshop for use in the water tray); set up role-play area around the outside water tray (e.g. café – pouring cups of tea, ice cream van – selling lollies and ice cream made from crushed, coloured ice).

- Use coloured water to enable children to see water levels in containers more easily.

- Plan regular adult input with a focus on encouraging talk and use of key vocabulary during investigations, and supporting individuals/groups of children in moving forward in identified areas.

- Make display more interactive, encouraging children to read pictures and signs, answer questions and respond to challenges. Change display more frequently. Link displays to children's current interests and investigations.

- Order the following resources: set of graded (tall narrow) measuring cylinders, small-world people and sea creatures, plastic lolly moulds, shallow storage baskets for permanent and additional resources. Organise and catalogue additional resources according to concept development.

Further points for discussion by foundation stage staff:

- What can children learn from observing other children's play?
- How can resources encourage problem solving?

Figure 6.2 cont

Recording and reporting

> Careful assessment and record-keeping underpin all good educational practice. They are essential elements in securing effective continuity and progression.
>
> (Department of Education and Science 1990)

Before making any decisions about record-keeping systems, practitioners should first consider the following questions:

- *Why* are we keeping records?
- *How* will the records be used?
- *Who* will contribute to/use the records?
- *What* will be included?
- *Which* is the most useful way of presenting and storing recorded information?

In answer to the first question, there are usually a number of reasons why practitioners keep records and these will probably include:

- To make sure that information is available to, and easily shared with, all concerned parties
- To enable practitioners to monitor, or plot, the progress of individuals or groups of children
- To ensure continuity for the child
- To enable practitioners to check that breadth and balance in the curriculum is being maintained
- In order to be accountable to e.g. the LEA, school management, OFSTED.

Records are used:

- As a 'central point' for the on-going collection of information and/or evidence
- As a source of reference when planning for individuals or the curriculum
- As evidence to support assessments or referrals
- To communicate information to parents
- To communicate information to other professionals
- To inform summative reporting.

Some records will be in daily use and need to be readily available at all times. Others will be accessed less frequently but all concerned parties should know where they are kept. There will be times when the content of records is of a sensitive nature, or is strictly confidential, and such information must be stored carefully to ensure that it is only available to its intended audience.

The obvious contributors to the records are the staff themselves, but practitioners should also consider how to include information from:

- Parents and carers
- Outside agencies (e.g. health visitors, speech therapists, GPs).

The suitability of record-keeping systems for use in early years settings will depend on the purpose of the record and its audience and contributors. Systems should be efficient and support, not hinder, practitioners in their role as educators. Time is a limited resource and a balance must be sought between recording observations and interacting with the children. Practitioners should set themselves realistic goals and only record what is useful. The next part of the chapter looks at some methods of recording and reporting information.

Individual profiles of children's work

The profiling system is in operation in many settings and can be a very successful way of combining observations and assessments made in the setting and in the home. The profile is started on the child's entry to the setting (often with a 'home visit' entry) and is an on-going and formative record of a child's achievements. The profile will be used by the practitioner in assessing and addressing individual learning needs and, as well as being informative and attractive to the child and parent, should be effective in supporting the planning and reporting process. Information should be presented in a logical way, and should be easily accessible and useful.

Compiling a profile

There are a variety of ways in which information can be organised in a profile. Some practitioners favour the diary format, making entries in chronological order regardless of the curricular content of the learning. Others prefer to organise information according to curricular focus. In the latter type of profile, there will be a section for each area of learning and entries will be made in chronological order within each section. This system has the advantage of showing clearly a child's progress in a particular area of learning but it can sometimes be difficult to decide in which section to include some cross-curricular entries.

In practical terms, the profile should be durable enough to withstand frequent handling over a considerable period of time. Entries can be made on sheets of paper which are then inserted into transparent plastic pockets and filed in a plastic-covered ring binder. Alternatively, a scrapbook could be used for entries and kept in an envelope file for protection. Practitioners will probably want to peruse the numerous stationery catalogues on the market before making a decision!

The content of the profile will include:

- Written observations
- Pieces of the child's work (e.g. mark-making, paintings)
- Photographs of children's work (perhaps work in progress, a 3D model, a physical activity such as riding a bike).

For examples of contents, see Figures 6.3, 6.4, 6.5, 6.6.

When making entries in the profiles, practitioners should adhere to the following guidance:

- The emphasis should be on what the child *can* do – the profile is a record of the child's *achievements*.
- Entries should be written objectively.
- All entries must be dated (including the year).

- Children's work and photographs should be annotated (e.g. notes made on area of provision in which the learning took place, analysis of learning, time span, adult/peer support received).
- When photographs or pieces of work relate to other written observations, there should be clear referencing.
- In the event of an extended period of absence, this should be recorded in the child's profile.
- Where possible, children should be involved in making entries (particularly own work and photographs).
- Practitioners should keep abreast of entries from home and add their own notes to these as appropriate.

Recording observations and assessments for profiles

Written observations can be recorded straight away in the profile, or can be written on large, white adhesive labels to be added to the profile later (Figure 6.3). It can be helpful to keep a stock of labels or pieces of paper, and a pen, in each area of provision – it is very frustrating, having anticipated a milestone achievement, to miss the 'magic moment' while in search of tools and equipment with which to record it! Some practitioners prefer to write in a personal notebook and transfer information to the profile – these written observations are sometimes cut out of the book and glued into the profile.

FOCUS AREA OF LEARNING: KNOWLEDGE AND UNDERSTANDING OF THE WORLD

<u>12th February 2000</u>
Today Sarah chose to work in the workshop and told Sandeep that she was going to make a kite. She selected the following materials and tools: tissue paper, 2 lolly sticks, string, glue, sellotape and scissors. Sarah cut the paper with the scissors and fastened it to the stick with sellotape (having tried and rejected the glue because it was "too wet"). As Sandeep held the kite, she fastened the string to it with sellotape. They took the finished kite outside and, pulling it behind her as she ran, Sarah shouted "Look! It's flying! The wind's blowing it!"

Figure 6.3 Adhesive label entry: 'Kite observation'

There are also times when observations will be recorded in a standard format. There are three clear purposes for using a framework within which to record observations and assessments:

- To support the practitioner in focusing observations and assessments
- To support the practitioner in organising the written content
- To enable the reader to more easily understand and use information.

When observing children in the setting, it can be physically difficult, and probably not necessary, to write down everything that is witnessed. Having access to a few carefully chosen headings on a sheet of paper will support the practitioner in selecting information to record. Information recorded on standard formats is easily accessed by colleagues who are also familiar with the format, and this shared understanding of the system will impact positively on the efficiency of team assessment and planning discussions.

Sometimes teams produce a simple pro forma on which to record observations during a planned activity. These can help practitioners to adhere to a specific observation focus and can, when completed, be stuck straight into the profile (see Figure 6.6). Practitioners will almost certainly find a standard annotation format useful, as illustrated in Figure 6.4. In the process of transferring jottings to such a framework, information will be organised in a more readable and logical form.

Name of child: **Cameron**	Date: **20th September, 2000**
Area of provision/focus activity: **Office area**	

Other contextual information:
Cameron worked alone in the area and unsupported by an adult.

Observed learning: (What did the child do and say? What does the child know and understand?)
Cameron entered the area very purposefully and selected a pencil and a piece of 'memo' paper. He made separate marks on the paper confidently, working from left to right until he had reached the bottom. He then read back his 'memo':

"I am going to the park. I am going with Billy (dog). I am taking the ball. I am taking the lemonade. I am taking the lead."

Cameron then attached the 'memo' to the message board and left the area.

Cameron understands that writing carries meaning, and that it can be used to communicate messages. He readily uses writing in his play and is showing an awareness of left to right orientation when making, and reading back, his marks.

Figure 6.4 'Memo': child's mark-making and adult's assessment using standard annotation pro forma

It will not, however, always be appropriate to use a pro forma for the recording of observations and sometimes a separate list of 'prompts' (as illustrated in the example 'Observation of Natasha', pp. 131–133), or a clear focus in the practitioner's mind, can be just as capable of effecting a coherent and useful record.

Although the reorganisation of some written material will be necessary (perhaps onto an annotation form), copying out long observations into profiles is an unproductive use of time and should be avoided where possible. Although children's work should always be presented in a respectful fashion, and entries neat and orderly, the profile is a working document and presentation should not take priority over content.

<u>28th June, 2000 (construction area)</u>

Isaac spent 20 minutes building a jungle with a group of children. He contributed lots of ideas during discussions about plans and use of materials. He suggested making a waterfall using blue cellophane and white crepe paper and when it was finished he commented "It looks splashy".

Isaac continued to play with the jungle for 10 minutes after the other children had left the area – he built a "sand mountain" (using a toy lorry and orange tissue paper) and a bridge so that the animals could "go and have their babies there". Isaac was keen to talk to Mrs R. about the jungle and introduced the animal characters to her before explaining where they all lived. He then went on to tell her about the small elephant's adventure (using the toy elephant to demonstrate actions):

"He was running, he lost his mummy. He went up the rocks and he fell down the waterfall. It was like a slide. Then he saw his mummy and he was happy."

Creative development: Isaac communicates imaginative ideas using materials and resources creatively. He is able to express his ideas verbally and uses them in 'story-making' play.

Figure 6.5
Jungle play in the construction area (see chapter 3, p. 62 for 'Jungle play' activity plan)

Profiles as 'shared records'

Young children's profiles are an on-going record of their achievements (from entering to leaving the setting) in all areas of learning and are often referred to as their 'special books'. Children should be encouraged to look at, and talk about, the contents and the learning it represents with friends, practitioners, parents and carers. For this reason, profiles should be made accessible (perhaps in book racks on the wall or open boxes), and should be easy to handle. They should be clearly named and ideally display a photograph of the child on the front so as to be instantly recognisable. When children feel 'ownership' of their profile, and a pride in their achievements, they will probably ask to make their own entries, sharing experiences from home as well as in the setting.

Although practitioners will have talked with parents about profiles (purpose and content) during the first contact period, it is a good idea to display a notice of explanation and encouragement, similar to the following example, close to where the profiles are kept.

Name: Jasmine	Date: 24th September, 1999

FOCUS ACTIVITY: 2D SHAPE TRAIL (circle, triangle, square, rectangle)

FOCUS AREA OF LEARNING: MATHEMATICAL DEVELOPMENT

Context/Response:
The activity took place around the inside and outside areas of the setting. Jasmine was keen to participate and chose to work with Sam. After some adult support (further explanation of activity and reassurance as they matched the first few shapes), the pair spent 10 minutes searching for shapes together. Each of the children had their own recording sheet.

Matching of shapes:
Jasmine confidently matched all 4 flat shapes when there was no difference in orientation to those on her sheet. She was able to recognise the triangle whatever its orientation.

Understanding/use of key vocabulary (shape names/size vocabulary):
Jasmine understood, and used correctly, the words 'circle' and 'triangle'. When asked to find a square, she was able to point at the correct shape. She referred to the rectangle (vertical presentation) as a 'door shape'. She used the words 'big' and 'small' spontaneously in her play and responded appropriately when asked to find a 'bigger/smaller' circle.

Use of recording sheet:
Jasmine used the sheet confidently and independently, making a mark in the appropriate space every time she found a shape. At the end of the trail, she took the record to Mr D. saying "Look how many I've got!" With support from Mr D., she counted the marks for each shape and decided that she had found more triangles than any other shape.

Figure 6.6 'Shape Trail': using a pro forma for recording observations during a planned focus activity (see chapter 2, p. 51 for 'Shape Trail' activity plan)

Children's Profiles – notice of explanation

The children's profiles are a celebration of their achievements and contain examples and photographs of work, and observations by nursery staff. They are intended to show learning in all areas:

- Personal, social and emotional development
- Communication, language and literacy
- Mathematical development
- Knowledge and understanding of the world
- Physical development
- Creative development.

Children learn in many different situations and places, and much of their learning takes place at home. Please use the profile to record significant home learning experiences, and 'landmark' achievements. This will help to give a fuller picture of your child's learning, and will enable staff to share achievements.

The profiles are always available and you are welcome to look through them at any time – your children will probably be only too happy to share theirs with you! The nursery staff regularly spend time looking at, and talking about, children's own profiles with them and are happy to discuss these records with you.

Class/group files

There will be some information that will need to be accessible to staff but which should not be readily available to all adults in the setting. A ring binder divided into sections, one for each child, will be useful for the storage of information such as personal details collected during first contact period, and will be less cumbersome than individual files. Record card index boxes are compact and can provide a practical and convenient storage system for home addresses, telephone numbers and contact names.

Tick lists

Tick lists as a method of recording information should be used with caution. A tick in a box against a statement or question is of limited value in communicating information about a child – children's learning rarely progresses in 'boxed' stages. If this method is used, it should be supported by observations that offer an explanation of context and a more accurate assessment of learning.

Sometimes it can be useful to transfer certain information from a number of observations onto one 'checklist' record sheet to give an overview of, for example, how many children observed playing in the home corner used the mark-making equipment in that area. This could help practitioners in assessing how provision is being used. It can also be useful to keep a 'tick-list' record of profile entries so that practitioners can see at a glance whether or not a child has been observed recently in a particular area of provision or learning.

Another circumstance in which the use of a tick-list might be justified is when children are required to register their presence in an area – this is often done by making a mark, or tick, next to their name. This type of record will only tell the practitioner that the child has been in the area, not what he or she has done or learnt.

Summative reporting

Teams should meet periodically to summarise children's achievements and to consider next steps (in some settings, this may be the responsibility of an individual practitioner). During such reviews, practitioners will make written records although it would be a daunting task to commit to paper all that they know about each child! Information and evidence collected in profiles and through other assessments should be used to inform practitioners and support them in producing an accurate summary.

In reporting upon children's progress to parents, the emphasis should be on informal discussion at regular intervals throughout the child's time in the setting. Written, summative reports to parents are not appropriate in all settings and, where they are required, should be in addition to the above-mentioned discussions. Reports should be written in a positive way, stressing the child's achievements and interests. The way in which content is organised in the report will vary between settings, although quite often practitioners categorise information in the six areas of learning. There may also be space allowed for an example of the child's work, comments from the child and parents, and for identifying 'next steps'. It will be necessary, as pointed out in chapter 4, to make time for discussion of the content of the report between parent and practitioner.

It is good practice, in the interests of continuity, to make communication links between settings, and practitioners should give careful consideration to what, and how, information is passed between professionals. Often, the written summative report will be sent on to the next setting. This system of reporting will be strengthened and supported if a more interactive approach to the 'passing on' of information is also in operation. Discussions between practitioners prior to the child's transition, and the sharing of profiles, can be very productive and illuminating.

Children frequently respond differently in new situations and unfamiliar surroundings. Their achievements will be affected by circumstances and environment and, because of this, practitioners will find it useful to refer to records and reports from settings previously attended by the child when making assessments within the first few weeks.

There is a requirement to provide quantifiable evidence of children's learning on entry to school and it is appropriate at this point to explain a little bit about 'baseline assessment', particularly with regard to the communication of information between settings. The aim of baseline assessment is to provide information (in the areas of communication, language and literacy, mathematical development and personal and social development) that will help reception staff to plan an appropriate curriculum and to record a starting point against which future progress can be measured. The assessment should take place within seven weeks of the child entering the reception class, and in the context of the usual classroom organisation and activities. In September 1998, it became a statutory requirement for all maintained primary schools to use one of the numerous baseline assessment schemes accredited by QCA. The criteria for accreditation include an obligation to offer guidance on how to use children's records from previous settings in assessing their attainment and to inform future planning. In making this specification, QCA have recognised the importance of the preschool experience in the assessment and planning process, and it is the challenge of the preschool practitioner to provide useful information about children's learning without allowing 'baseline' standards to dictate the curriculum. Further information about baseline assessment is available from the QCA (see also the website at: http://www.qca.org.uk/baseline).

In concluding this chapter, the following extract from Mary Jane Drummond's book *Assessing Children's Learning* is offered as a summary of the purpose and role of assessment in the foundation stage:

> In assessment, we can appreciate and understand what children learn; we can recognise their achievements, and their individuality, the differences between them. We can use our assessments to shape and enrich our curriculum, our interactions, our provision as a whole; we can use our assessments as a way of identifying what children will be able to learn next, so that we can support and extend that learning. Assessment is part of our daily practice in striving for quality.

(Drummond 1993)

CHAPTER 7

Looking forward

Having looked at planning for children's current learning needs and interests, and discussed long-term curricular planning in detail, it now remains for the reader to look to the future and consider how best to plan the way forward for the setting and the team.

The content of this chapter is organised as follows:

- Moving forward with colleagues (p. 145)
- Development planning (p. 146)
- Action planning (p. 147)
- Post-inspection action plans (p. 147)

Moving forward with colleagues

Good teamwork is essential if a setting is to provide a rich and secure environment for young children, and to make positive steps forward. All staff should be purposefully involved in discussions and decision making about curricular and organisational issues, and about long-term developments. Such involvement will encourage attitudes of commitment and self-confidence, and will ensure a firm understanding of the aims of the setting by all staff, irrespective of background or current responsibilities.

There is much to be gained from the sharing of knowledge and ideas between colleagues. The strengths, skills, training and experience of all individuals should be valued and used positively to enrich and fortify the team as a whole. Roles should be complementary, not conflicting, and teams built on a foundation of:

- Communication
- Cooperation
- Respect
- Support.

Communication between practitioners need not be restricted to the immediate team within which individuals work on a day-to-day basis. Indeed there are many childminders who spend much of their working time as the only adult with a group of children. The wider 'network' of practitioners offers a rich source of professional support. Inter-setting meetings, or visits to other settings during the working day, can prove to be both informative and stimulating. Meetings may be used as a forum for the sharing of good practice or the discussion of new initiatives, legislation and policies; practitioners can decide their own agenda, addressing issues of interest or concern.

In order to build a 'balanced' team with expertise and knowledge across a range of areas, a programme of professional development for staff will need to be planned. This programme should allow scope for individual professional interests to be developed, as well as addressing the needs of the whole team and setting. This is an area that should be considered in the long term so that all needs are coordinated and met over a period of time. Professional development can take a number of forms and practitioners will make judgements regarding suitability according to the content of the learning, the prior training and experience of the individual or individuals involved, the convenience of the timings (e.g. organisation of staff release time or cover) and cost. However, it should be said that, if a team has a serious commitment to staff development, and a clear view of the way forward, every effort will be made to find appropriate routes for development. It is a good idea to 'appoint' a member of the team as the person responsible for collating and presenting information about professional development opportunities. It may be that the local education authority offers courses or workshops tailored to the identified needs of the team, or arranged visits to, for example, other agencies to learn about services offered may be more useful.

Development planning

Practitioners should be constantly evaluating the service that is offered to children and parents, looking for ways to develop the setting. It is never possible to sit back and think that the job of planning for young children's learning is complete; a 'static' setting is inevitably a stale environment, unlikely to inspire children or adults. Development is about:

- Evolving   • Growing   • Advancing.

Some decisions regarding improvements will be made from day to day, and others as immediate needs arise but, in order to organise and integrate the needs and successfully effect improvements, practitioners will need to agree a longer-term plan for development. This plan will identify where the setting is at the starting point, and where practitioners intend it to be at the end of, for example, three years. It will broadly outline steps to be taken, and changes to be made, during that period. Development planning can be used to address issues such as curriculum development, staff development, organisation of staffing, building maintenance and alterations, and is about having a 'vision' for the future of the setting.

There will probably be many potential areas for development and prioritising can be difficult. Some will obviously be urgent and will take priority, others will have to be 'put on hold' or scheduled for a later date. Sometimes a weakness will have been identified and the relevant area targeted for improvement, in other cases, practitioners will plan to build on successes. It is important to be realistic and guard against trying to tackle too much in a short space of time; targets should be manageable and organised in a time sequence.

When making decisions, practitioners should take into account factors such as the following:

- Financial constraints
- Expertise available
- Introduction of e.g. new Government requirements

- Communication systems
- Time constraints
- Other responsibilities and commitments.

Although plans will span a period of up to five years, they should be viewed as working documents and reviewed and amended in progress. For example, at the end of year 1 in a three-year plan, practitioners should evaluate success revising the plan as necessary for years 2 and 3, and perhaps adding targets for an additional year.

Action planning

Through the process of development planning, practitioners make decisions about *what* needs to be done in order to move the setting forward. Action planning is the process by which they clarify *how* improvements will be realised in practice. For example, practitioners may take an area targeted for development and draw up a programme of action for the forthcoming year. In their plan they will define:

- Key issue
- Objectives
- Action to be taken
- Roles and responsibilities
- Resource implications
- Criteria for success
- Monitoring success: responsibilities and methods
- Time scales.

If a plan is to be implemented smoothly, all involved adults will need to be part of the planning process throughout and should fully understand their responsibilities. A commitment from all parties is necessary in order to ensure a successful outcome within the allotted period of time.

Post-inspection action plans

Post-inspection action plans are about making improvements in areas where weaknesses have been identified during an OFSTED inspection. It may be that some of the issues for concern have already been recognised by the practitioner, or team of practitioners, and steps taken to address them. However, settings are required to draw up a 'post-inspection action plan' within 40 working days of receipt of the report. This is a statement of how the practitioner intends to address the key issues identified during the inspection. It will probably include short-, medium- and long-term intentions and should aim to have successfully achieved all targets within a year. Teams are obliged to provide the LEA with a copy of the plan if requested.

Foundation-stage practitioners find themselves in a period of significant change and it is to their credit that they embrace initiatives with commitment and an open mind. However, in striving to keep abreast of developments in local and national policy, and to be practising in accordance with current thinking, it is easy to lose direction or cohesion as a team. Practitioners should give priority to developing a shared ethos and, above all, they need to invest in time for talking and listening to each other.

> Working as a team is a process not a technique. It is rooted in an ideology of empowerment, encouraging adults (whether parents or staff) to take control of their own lives and giving children permission to do the same.

(Whalley 1996)

Bibliography

Abbott, L. and Rodger, R. (eds) (1994) *Quality Education in the Early Years.* Buckingham: Open University Press.

Anning, A. (1999) *Promoting Children's Learning from Birth to Five: Developing the New Early Years Professional.* Buckingham: Open University Press.

Anning, A. (ed.) (1994) *The First Years at School.* Buckingham: Open University Press.

Athey, C. (1990) *Extending Thought in Young Children: A Parent–Teacher Partnership.* London: Paul Chapman Publishing.

Bennett, N. *et al.* (1997) *Teaching Through Play: Teachers' Thinking and Classroom Practice.* Buckingham: Open University Press.

Blenkin, G. M. and Kelly, A.V. (eds) (1992) *Assessment in Early Childhood Education.* London: Paul Chapman Publishing.

Blenkin, G. M. and Kelly, A. V. (eds) (1996) *Early Childhood Education: A Developmental Curriculum,* 2nd edn. London: Paul Chapman Publishing.

Bruce, T. (1987) *Early Childhood Education.* London: Hodder and Stoughton.

Bruce, T. (1997) *Early Childhood Education,* 2nd edn. London: Hodder and Stoughton.

Chapman, L. (1978) *Approaches to Art in Education.* New York: Harcourt Brace Jovanovich.

Cullingford, C. (1997) *Assessment Versus Evaluation.* London: Cassell.

Curtis, A. (1998) *A Curriculum for the Preschool Child,* 2nd edn. London: Routledge.

David, T. (1990) *Under five – Under Educated?* Buckingham: Open University Press.

Department of Education and Science (1967) *Children and their Primary Schools: A Report of the Central Advisory Council for Education (England).* London: HMSO (The Plowden Report).

Department for Education and Science (1990) *Starting with Quality: The Report of the Committee of Inquiry into the Quality of Educational Experience offered to 3- and 4-year olds.* London: HMSO (The Rumbold Report).

Drummond, M. J. (1993) *Assessing Children's Learning.* London: David Fulton Publishers.

Duffy, B. (1998) *Supporting Creativity and Imagination in the Early Years.* Buckingham: Open University Press.

Edington, M. (1998) *The Nursery Teacher in Action.* London: Paul Chapman Publishing.

Fisher, J. (1996) *Starting from the Child?* Buckingham: Open University Press.

Fisher, R. (1990) *Teaching Children to Think.* Oxford: Basil Blackwell (reprinted in 1995, Cheltenham: Stanley Thornes).

Hall, N. (1987) *The Emergence of Literacy.* London: Hodder and Stoughton.

Hurst, V. (1991) *Planning for Early Learning: Education in the First Five Years.* London: Paul Chapman Publishing.

Hurst, V. and Lally, M. (1992) 'Assessment and the nursery curriculum', in Blenkin, G. M. and Kelly, A. V. (eds) *Assessment in Early Childhood Education*, ch. 3. London: Paul Chapman Publishing.

Isaacs, S. (1929) *The Nursery Years: The Mind of the Child from Birth to Six Years*. London: Routledge and Kegan Paul.

Kress, G. (1997) *Before Writing: Rethinking the Paths to Literacy*. London: Routledge.

Lancaster, J. (ed.) (1987) *Art, Craft and Design in the Primary School,* 2nd edn. Corsham: National Society for Education in Art and Design (NSEAD).

Lindon, J. (1997) *Working with Young Children,* 3rd edn. London: Hodder and Stoughton.

Lindsay, G. and Desforges, M. (1998) *Baseline Assessment: Practice, Problems and Possibilities*. London: David Fulton Publishers.

Moyles, J. R. (1989) *Just Playing*. Buckingham: Open University Press.

Moyles, J. R. (1994) *The Excellence of Play*. Buckingham: Open University Press.

Nutbrown, C. (1999) *Threads of Thinking,* 2nd edn. London: Paul Chapman Publishing.

Office for Standards in Education (1999) *Handbook for Inspecting Primary and Nursery Schools with guidance on self-evaluation*. London: OFSTED.

Office for Standards in Education (2000a) *Are You Ready for Inspection? A Guide for Nursery Education Providers in the Private, Voluntary and Independent Sectors*. London: OFSTED.

Office for Standards in Education (2000b) *Handbook for Inspecting Nursery Education in the Private, Voluntary and Independent Sectors including the Inspection Framework*. London: OFSTED.

Piaget, J. (1962) *Play, Dreams and Imitation in Childhood*. London: Routledge and Kegan Paul.

Perry, R. (1997) *Teaching Practice – A Guide for Early Childhood Students*. London: Routledge.

QCA (1999) *Early Learning Goals*. London: Qualifications and Curriculum Authority.

QCA (2000) *Curriculum Guidance for the Foundation Stage*. London: Qualifications and Curriculum Authority.

Whalley, M. (1996) 'Working as a team', in Pugh, G. (ed.) *Contemporary Issues in the Early Years: Working Collaboratively for Children*. London: Paul Chapman Publishing.

Whitebread, D. (ed.) (1996) *Teaching and Learning in the Early Years*. London: Routledge.

Index